Do I
Really Need a
Lawyer?

STUART KAHAN
ROBERT M. CAVALLO, B.S., J.D.
Co-author and Legal Consultant

Do I
Really Need a
Lawyer?

A FRANK E. TAYLOR BOOK
Chilton Book Company
RADNOR, PENNSYLVANIA

52812

Library of Congress Cataloging in Publication Data
Kahan, Stuart.
    Do I really need a lawyer?

    "A Frank E. Taylor book."
    Includes index.
    1. Law—United States—Popular works.   I. Cavallo,
Robert M., joint author.   II. Title.
KF387.K28   340'.0973   78-14636
ISBN 0-8019-6775-9

A Frank E. Taylor Book

1 2 3 4 5 6 7 8 9 0   8 7 6 5 4 3 2 1 0 9

Contents

Introduction   1

1 Consumer Protection   4

Warranties   6
Local Legislative Control   7
Federal Regulatory Agencies   9
You and Credit   11
You and the Credit Bureau   15
To Complain   16
Product Liability   17
To Summarize   18

2 Human Rights   19

Your Basic Rights   19
Defamation   21
Invasion of Privacy   22
Equal Opportunities   24
  Employment   24
  Housing   27
  Credit   27
Changing Your Name   28
To Summarize   28

3   Family Matters   29

Marriage   29
Children   32
Adoptions   32
Separation and Divorce   35
To Summarize   43

4   Real Property Transactions   44

Renting   44
Buying and Selling   50
Condominiums   55
Cooperatives   57
To Summarize   59

5   Business Relationships   60

Individual Ownership   60
Partnerships   61
Corporations   63
Terminating a Business   65
Bankruptcy   66
Copyrights, patents, and trademarks   67
To Summarize   69

6   Crimes and Other Offenses   70

Your Rights   70
Bail   72
Hearings   72
Arrest and Search Warrants   76
Small Criminal Complaints   78
To Summarize   79

7   Negligence and Malpractice   81

The Automobile   81
The Home   87
Legal fees   90
Medical Malpractice   91
To Summarize   94

8   Wills   95

The Benefits of a Will   97
Requirements for a Valid Will   99
Making a Will   99
The Executor   100
Planning Your Estate   101
Alternatives to a Will   102
Challenging a Will   105
To Summarize   106

9   The Courts and How They Work   108

The Federal Courts   108
The State Courts   110
Small Claims Court   112
Arbitration   116
To Summarize   119

10   Selecting a Lawyer   120

Canons of Ethics   122
The Types of Lawyers   128
Legal Fees   131
What Results to Expect   135
To Summarize   137
In Conclusion   138

Appendix   139

Index   188

Do I
Really Need a
Lawyer?

Introduction

"I was crossing Main and Elm in my new car when another guy ran the stop sign and rammed into me. My car was totaled. I was taken to the hospital with a broken arm. The other guy says that no-fault insurance will pay for everything. Does no-fault apply? Do I need a lawyer anyway?"

"My wife and I are splitting up. It's amicable, and we've pretty much agreed on child-support payments and the custody of the children. Can't we just put all this down on paper without a lawyer?"

"I've got $2,000 in the bank, but I owe some $25,000 for the bakery which went under. I don't know how I can ever pay those creditors. Maybe I should declare bankruptcy. I hear it's easy to do and that I don't really need a lawyer, which I can't afford anyway. Is it that easy to do?"

"I'm taking my cleaner to the cleaners—to court, that is. He ruined my new coat. I only wore it twice. He owes me $275, the price of the coat. Do I have to bring a lawyer with me?"

"My friends say it is a waste of money to have a lawyer draw a will for me. They say that I can easily do it myself by writing it out on a piece of paper and having someone witness my signature. Is this true?"

"We are buying a condominium in Florida. Most of our friends are now down there. They tell us the arrangement is a simple one. The owner-developer has a standard contract. One bank in the area issues all the

1

mortgages. It's all supposed to be cut-and-dried. So, do we really need a lawyer?"

These are but a few of the many problems the average person may encounter in everyday life, and their resolutions all center around the question of whether or not legal representation is needed.

Felix Frankfurter once said, "Our society . . . is a legal state in the sense that almost everything that takes place will sooner or later raise legal questions." Lawyers are an integral part of our "legal state"—in fact, of our very existence. Lawyer-politicians represent us at every stage of public policy-making: indeed, more than half the members of Congress and almost a quarter of our state legislators are lawyers. Trial lawyers in the headlines demand our attention. Indeed, concern with laws and law-making seems to permeate every stage of our lives.

In the past fifteen years the number of lawyers in the United States has increased from 300,000 to 475,000. Law-school enrollments have more than doubled; now they number more than 125,000. And women are entering the profession in greater numbers. Ten years ago women accounted for only 5 percent of law-school enrollment; today they represent 25 percent of that enrollment, and at a few schools the figure is as high as 50 percent.

The image of the lawyer has been tarnished of late. Watergate has seen to that. But, although there may be a few bad apples in a barrel, most of them are good. And the truth is that because of the availability of lawyers to everyone, the United States maintains one of the most accessible court systems with one of the most exhaustive lists of human rights in the world.

The intention of this book is not to teach you law, but to illuminate some of those rights, to point out many common and uncommon legal problems, and to furnish guidelines so that you can make a judgment, based on solid information, of your own legal needs. It is not our intention to tell you what you should or should not do. We simply want to enable you to make intelligent decisions. This book, then, is *not* an alternative to a lawyer, nor is it a do-it-yourself kit.

In our research we have drawn on a national survey undertaken by a special committee of the American Bar Association in collaboration with the American Bar Foundation to discover the legal needs of the public. The purpose of this survey was to elicit information about the legal problems encountered by the public, how those problems have been handled, the public's experiences with lawyers, and its opinions and perceptions about lawyers and their work. The planning of this study began in 1971; more than 2,000 persons were interviewed in great depth. The report was released in 1977 ("The Legal Needs of the Public"/ABA), and we cite some of the statistics in these pages.

And we have conducted interviews of our own with scores of people across the country. Judges, lawyers, and legal researchers were consulted, in addition to nonprofessionals. A number of questions were asked, including (1) what is the public's concern regarding a specific area or areas of the law? (2) Is a lawyer necessary in all instances? If not, what can the layman do? (3) If a lawyer is necessary, how can the layman find the right one? (4) What will the lawyer cost? (5) What will the lawyer do? (6) What results can be reasonably expected?

We now pass those findings on to you.

The Appendix in the back of the book has been compiled in order to provide you with a useful and handy guide regarding state laws and regulations. The Appendix also contains samples of various legal forms and includes listings of agencies and organizations—federal, state, and local—to whom you can write for advice or to whom you can file a complaint regarding discrimination or any other violation of your rights.

It should be noted here that throughout the book the terms *lawyer* and *attorney* are used interchangeably, and we refer to the lawyer as "he" only in the interests of readability.

1

Consumer Protection

In the past, the buyer and the seller traded across the table. The seller gave his best sales pitch, and the buyer in turn gave his best "No." It was an era of *Caveat Emptor*, or "let the buyer beware," and it was up to the buyer to separate malarky from truth. In effect, the seller took no responsibility for what he sold you; he simply left town.

Today, the situation is quite different. The seller now is held responsible for much of what he says. He is still allowed a certain amount of sales pitch, such as telling you that a particular washing machine is a "tremendous buy," but if he says that "it will last for forty years," that is his opinion, and he may have to stand behind it. What it comes down to is that when the seller makes a promise, he makes a warranty (a guarantee of the integrity of the product), and under the law he is responsible.

As soon as you buy something, you create a contract by virtue of the sale purchase of the item involved. Basically, the law of sales is governed by two specific statutes: the Uniform Sales Act, adopted by thirty-eight states, and the Uniform Commerical Code, adopted by forty-nine states, Louisiana being the exception. However, the intention here is not to teach you the law but rather to answer the question as to whether you really need a lawyer. But first, some practical background would be helpful.

When you go into a record store and ask the clerk for an album, or when you order an album by phone (or in fact in any other way where you place an order and it is accepted), you are entering into a *contract of sale.* But when you visit a boat showroom and give the salesman an order for a Chris Craft 25-footer with twin outboards, and he doesn't have that particular model in stock but agrees to get it for you, then you are entering into a *contract to buy.*

Therefore you should know how those contracts can be protected in your state; so, the first question is whether or not the contract you plan to enter into *must* be a written one. Many laws have been enacted and many governmental agencies have been formed to protect the consumer from unfair and fraudulent business practices.

For example, in most jurisdictions, if you agree to buy certain items over the sum of $500, the agreement to buy *must be in writing.* And, if you agree to purchase land, *that* agreement must be a written one. Also, contracts calling for services to be rendered to you, and where those services cannot be performed within one year, must be in writing.

In addition, certain contracts are not permissible at all on the basis that they are against public policy; that is, against the public good. In most states, with the exception of Nevada and New Jersey, gambling contracts are illegal and deemed void. Moreover, contracts stipulating interest rates beyond those set forth under state law are also not valid.

And it doesn't stop with these examples. Age is a factor, too. In some states, you are considered an adult when you reach the age of eighteen. Therefore if you are seventeen and purchase a bicycle, the contract cannot be enforced against either you or your parents, if, for instance, you haven't paid for it, and the bicycle must be returned to the seller. If you bought the bike at seventeen and at eighteen still retained possession of it, that factor alone may be deemed a ratification, and therefore any action by the seller *could* be maintained against you.

The first rule then to consider is this: Inasmuch as laws vary from state to state, if there is a question of ownership, it is best to consult a lawyer. For example, you go to your local sewing center and buy a dual-bobbin sewing machine with an automatic buttonhole-maker. But you haven't set up your sewing room yet. So, you leave the machine at the store for the time being. The store burns down one night and your machine with it. What happens? You're out one sewing machine because ownership passed to you at the moment you bought it.

But suppose the sewing machine was a secondhand one and repairs were necessary in order to put it in working condition? Now comes the fire. You're *not* out one sewing machine because the dealer retained ownership until the appropriate repairs were made.

Or suppose the dealer gives you the option of returning the machine after a week's trial period instead of paying for it. While the machine is in your possession, a robber breaks into your home one night and takes your color television set, your quadraphonic stereo, and your sewing machine. Who's out now? Actually, when the dealer gave you the machine, ownership passed to you. If you decided after the week that you didn't like the machine, ownership would pass again to the dealer. While it was in your possession, though, it was stolen. You have no recourse.

However, if your agreement with the dealer was for him to deliver the sewing machine "on approval," then ownership passed to you when you indicated your approval or when you retained the machine beyond what was considered a reasonable period of time without giving notice of dissatisfaction.

Confusing? As you can see, there are many variables. Obviously it isn't necessary to consult a lawyer when you buy a sewing machine, but the point to remember is that the laws of your state may dictate certain policies, and if you are buying a high-ticket item, such as a car or boat, you should make sure you know what the consequences will be under certain conditions.

This brings us logically to the legal protection that is afforded you, the consumer, today. The American Bar Association survey showed that for every 1,000 adults, 140 have a dispute on a major purchase, 50 have disputes with creditors, 30 are subject to repossession, and another 30 are subject to garnishment.

WARRANTIES

To a great extent unscrupulous manufacturers, dealers, and salesmen are held responsible today under statutes for a wide variety of conduct for which there previously were few legal remedies.

Although many laws have been enacted to protect you as a purchaser, you should be familiar with two basic warranties. One is an *express warranty*, which is actually an explicit written statement from the manufacturer or retailer guaranteeing the performance of the goods. For example, "XYZ Company warrants this unit to be free from defects in material and workmanship and will replace this unit or any defective part thereof free." The other is an *implied warranty*—and this is implicit in the sale of all consumer goods—which states that the goods are fit for the standard purposes for which they are sold and that they are free from defects.

The Federal Trade Commission, an agency that sets nationwide standards for warranties to prevent deceptive sales practices, states that warranties for consumer products must be in simple, concise language and must appear in a conspicuous place on the product. The warranty must also state who is guaranteeing the product, the time limits of the warranty, how to enforce it, and what is actually covered. Also, the steps one must take to repair the warranted product must be reasonable. This means that if the item cannot be satisfactorily repaired within a reasonable period of time, the purchase price must be refunded.

However, even all these protections may not be enough. Many sellers still make false claims in their advertising, and because of this considerable legislation has been enacted by various jurisdictions.

LOCAL LEGISLATIVE CONTROL

In addition to certain national laws, most states have enacted special laws to prevent deceptive trade practices. Here is what they are trying to control:

* Representing goods or services as being those of another entity or individual, or misrepresenting the source, sponsorship, approval, or certification of those goods. In effect, the seller is lying.
* Deceptive representations of geographic origins in connection with the goods or services; in other words, passing off goods as being made in London when they were really made in Afghanistan.
* Representing goods or services as having sponsorship approval or certain characteristics, ingredients, uses, benefits, or qualities that they do not have, or that the seller has sponsorship approval or affiliation that he does not have. This covers instances where one implies that he has the Good Housekeeping Seal of Approval when he does not.
* Representing the goods as original or new when in fact they are reconditioned, used, or secondhand. The classic cases are the rebuilt television set and the recapped tire.
* Representing the goods or services as being of a particular standard: calling them Grade A when they are really Grade Z; or goods that are supposed to be a particular style or model and are not.
* Denigrating the goods, services, or business of another by misrepresenting facts: "He sells defective merchandise. I do not. He sells used stuff. I do not. His merchandise is hot. Mind is not."
* Advertising goods or services with the intent of *not* selling them as advertised. The seller lists certain items at $1.98, but when you reach the

store, you find that they're being sold at $5.98. This is clearly false advertising; you are enticed into the store under a false pretence.

* Advertising goods or services without the intent of supplying reasonable, expectable demands; a big banner states that the Ajax Hardware Store is selling drills on Saturday morning for $7.00, but when the crowd descends upon Ajax, it finds that only three drills are for sale at that price, but that a different drill can be bought for $16. In effect, Ajax was inducing buyers to come forth in order to sell a more expensive item. This is known as "Bait and Switch," and it's illegal.

Another classic case is the restaurant that advertises two-for-the-price-of-one dinners on Monday night, but when you arrive with your spouse you find that the two-for-one applies only to a party of sixteen.

* Making dishonest or misleading statements of fact concerning the reasons for existence of or the amounts of price reductions. Typical of this is the "going-out-of-business" sale, where "we must sell," when in fact there is no intention of closing the doors. As an example, an outfit on Market Street in Philadelphia has been going out of business now for two years. It's in the business of going out of business.

* Representing that a product confers rights, remedies, or obligations that it does not or which are prohibited by law. "This little gadget makes it unnecessary to ever have to pay your phone bill again."

* Representing that a part, replacement, or repair service is needed when it is not. An example is the burned-out television tube trick. You are told that the set must be taken to the shop for extensive repairs—to the tune of $136—and that doesn't include the replacement tube.

* Representing that the subject of a transaction has already been supplied when in fact it has not. For example, after the guy has put up your aluminum siding, he installs gutters, claiming that under a previous deal you have already received your leaders.

* Representing that the consumer will receive a rebate, discount, or other benefit, and then he receives nothing because of some technicality. An example is misrepresentation as to the authority of the salesman, representative, or agent to negotiate the final terms of the transaction. In other words, you make a great deal for a car with a new salesman, but the dealer attempts to quash the arrangement because it was "too good"—for you, that is.

If you have been the victim of deceptive practices such as these, you can complain to the appropriate authority in your state or jurisdiction; either to the attorney general, the district attorney, or a specific consumer-protection agency. The person committing the infraction may be forced not only to rebate all sums of money paid by you but also may be slapped with a fine or with punitive damages.

Many states have also set up rules and regulations concerning particular occupations or professions. Licensing agencies of the states usually control attorneys, barbers, engineers, funeral directors, optometrists, chiropodists, psychologists, medical doctors, nurses, laboratory technicians, and the like. In fact, states now also regulate banks, loan companies, and insurance companies. If you have any grievance as to a billing or procedure, check your telephone book for the particular licensing agency in your jurisdiction and call to see if they do in fact license the individual who committed the infraction. If so, they will tell you how to register a complaint. For example, the Grievance Committee of the New York State Bar Association is particularly sensitive to complaints or inquiries made by any resident of the state against a particular attorney or attorneys. Normally a complaint or an inquiry causes an investigation by that licensing agent into the acts, misacts, and even nonacts against the party of whom you are complaining. If you cannot locate the appropriate licensing agency in your phone book, write to your Secretary of State in your state capital for the information.

With respect to electrical power and telephone and telegraphic communications, you can complain to the state public-utility commissions that regulate those businesses.

All these methods of course can be used without an attorney. (See the Appendix for a listing of consumer-protection organizations. Consult your telephone directory for additional names.)

FEDERAL REGULATORY AGENCIES

Many federal laws protect the consumer in areas where the state agencies may not have jurisdiction. These laws primarily cover goods that are part of interstate commerce; that is, transported from state to state. The two major ones are the Federal Trade Commission and the Food and Drug Administration.

The Federal Trade Commission (FTC) is composed of five commissioners appointed by the President with the advice and consent of the Senate; no more than three of the commissioners may be selected from the same political party. The FTC is not private; it is charged to act in behalf of the public. It was set up to prevent the use of "unfair methods of competition in commerce and unfair or deceptive acts or practices in commerce." It also investigates and regulates antitrust activity and is responsible for maintaining truth in lending and truth in advertising.

If you have a complaint within its jurisdiction, you can make it to the FTC in Washington or to a local branch. They will begin an investigation, and, if necessary, they will commence *all* regulatory proceedings against the offending party. In this case, you don't need a lawyer.

The Food and Drug Administration (FDA), a law enforcement agency within the Department of Health, Education, and Welfare, is generally responsible for regulating and maintaining food and drug laws; in other words, its function is to protect you from foods and drugs—even cosmetics—that might be harmful. It is also charged with the duty of removing unsafe products from the marketplace.

If you have any problem concerning drugs or health-related items, you can direct your inquiry to the FDA in Washington or to the branch in your local area for action. Again, no lawyer is needed.

Another federal law, the Magnuson-Moss Warranty Act, gives consumers some additional protection. It requires manufacturers who offer warranties on their products to specify what type of warranty is provided, either limited or full. Each product then must be labeled with the warranty. This law sets strict requirements for all products covered by a full warranty. Probably for this reason alone, you won't find too many full warranties today. But if you purchase a product with a limited warranty, be sure to read it carefully so you'll know its exact terms. This law also helps consumers bring lawsuits against manufacturers for failure to honor warranties or service contracts. In fact, under certain conditions the law even provides for paying the lawyers' fees in such actions. Of course it is not recommended that you bring large, involved actions against manufacturers without the aid of an attorney.

With respect to situations where you are ripped off by an unscrupulous vendor, there are agencies (state, local, and federal) that can come to your side. No attorney is necessary for most of the remedies being sought. Why? Because included in these governmental agencies are certain enforcement procedures to help the consumer seek the return of his monies or possibly to receive punitive damages. *Punitive damages* are money payments required of the offending party over and above the costs of the merchandise. This is a form of punishment, a kind of warning—and an expensive one at that—to him not to do it again.

Other consumer areas relate to the environment: to the air we breathe, the water we drink, and what rights we have as consumers.

In 1970 the Federal government passed the National Environmental

Protection Act, which required all governmental agencies to minimize the environmental harm under their aegis and to list in detail the environmental impact of each of their proposals. Various state and local agencies also have laws in the areas of air and water pollution and some even have laws on noise pollution. The scope and impact of these laws vary from community to community and are based mostly on need and political climate at the time they were passed. Thus the air pollution laws in New York City may be quite different from those in Wyoming. And, it may be illegal to blow your horn in Los Angeles (except for immediate danger), while in the Mohave Desert, who cares?

Implemented in the law are ways for the consumer to have certain wrongs righted without the help of an attorney. For example, if you live in Dallas and look out the window and see noxious black fumes emanating from a smokestack, you can call your local environmental protection agency. Most of these organizations are staffed with investigators, and upon your complaint they will inspect the offending premises and in many instances, if the offense proves to be in violation of the law, will issue subpoenas or summonses in order to prevent the pollution from continuing.

Incidentally, the fines for such abuses can be quite substantial: For example, a $25,000 violation relating to water pollution in the state of Alaska is not unusual. There are heavy penalties in other areas as well for violation of air pollution regulations. Most states do have regulatory agencies to handle various complaints.

YOU AND CREDIT

We've often heard the phrase "we live in a plastic society," and this could easily refer to credit cards. This plastic "money" accounts for more financial transactions in this country than Planters has peanuts, and it has brought forth such a buying surge that the federal government (which has traditionally been slow to react to the abuses of consumer groups) in 1968 enacted the Consumer Protection Credit Act, commonly known as the Truth-in-Lending Act. For the first time the cost of borrowing had to be set forth up front to the consumer. This act requires all lenders of money to spell out clearly the true interest costs and finance charges to be **paid** for a specific loan. In effect, you must be informed of the *exact* **charges** for credit, and those charges must be translated into an annual percentage rate of interest. But it doesn't stop here. The cost of credit must be printed in bold type and must appear on all monthly statements. In short, the lender cannot conceal finance charges, and he must tell the consumer what savings can be had if he pays the full amount at once. A lender therefore must inform the consumer of the method of his billing. He can charge interest on the consumer's previous balance or on an adjusted balance, but he cannot hide extra charges; thus items such as insurance and interest on insurance loans must be made known to the consumer.

Here's what happens: You go to your favorite department store and buy a sweater with your credit card. When you receive the statement from the store, it will include the terms of borrowing. This is generally known as the Retail Installment Credit Agreement, and it reads:

RETAIL INSTALLMENT CREDIT AGREEMENT

In consideration of our extending credit to you at our option, from time to time, you agree with us regarding all purchases made by you or others authorized to use your account: To pay us either: (a) the entire amount of your account within 30 days from the date of each monthly billing statement WITHOUT FINANCE CHARGE for that month, or at your option, (b) at least one-fifth of your new unpaid balance (but not less than $15) upon receipt of each monthly billing statement, together with a FINANCE CHARGE at the periodic rate of 1.5% per month on the first $500 of the Adjusted Balance (previous balance minus payments and credits) and 1% per month of any such balance in excess of $500. Minimum FINANCE CHARGE 50 cents on balance of $10 to $33. THE ANNUAL PERCENTAGE RATE determined by multiplying the periodic rate by 12 is 18% on the first $500 and 12% on the amount in excess of $500. In Pennsylvania, the ANNUAL PERCENTAGE RATE is 15%, determined by multiplying the periodic rate of 1.25% per month by 12. Minimum FINANCE CHARGE is 50 cents on Adjusted Balance of $10 to $40.

The Company may at any time amend any of the terms of this agreement upon written notice to buyer(s) of not less than 30 days. Credit cards issued under this agreement remain the property of the Company and must be surrendered upon request.

Buyer(s) authorizes the Company to report to proper persons and credit reporting agencies buyer(s) performance of this agreement.

We may declare your entire indebtedness hereunder to be due and payable if you default in making any payment hereunder in full when due, and we may charge reasonable attorney's fees not in excess of 20% of the amount due and payable under this agreement if it is referred to an attorney for collection. In New Jersey, such charge will not exceed 20% of the first $500 and 10% of any excess so payable. NOTICE TO THE BUYER. 1. YOU MAY AT ANY TIME PAY YOUR TOTAL INDEBTEDNESS UNDER THIS AGREEMENT. 2. DO NOT SIGN THIS AGREEMENT BEFORE YOU READ IT OR IF IT CONTAINS ANY BLANK SPACES. 3. YOU ARE ENTITLED TO A COMPLETELY FILLED-IN COPY OF THIS CREDIT AGREEMENT.

One of the major abuses of loan contracts has been the "balloon payment." This is a *final* payment, and it is considerably larger than the installment payments you, the debtor, have been making. Truth-in-Lending provides that if there is a balloon payment, it must be in large, bold type in any loan contract, and there must be a clause stating that there are methods available to refinance it.

Many states have laws controlling retail-installment sales or retail-credit sales. Some states have adopted what is known as the Uniform Consumer Credit Act whereas other states have their own laws. However, these apply only to retail-installment sales for goods and services to consumers. State consumer-credit laws make many of the same demands on the lenders as the Truth-in-Lending Act: (1) all costs and terms of credit must be revealed to the consumer, (2) there can be no blank spots in the contract, and (3) the print on the contract must be large, with the finance charges in even bolder print than the rest of the contract.

The Truth-in-Lending Act applies to practically all consumer-credit transactions, whether you are charging a purchase or borrowing cash. In fact, all conditions must be revealed to you before you even open a charge account. For example, you must be told how the finance charge is to be determined, how long you have to pay it, and the minimum payment required. Also, the following information must be included in your monthly statement: (1) your previous balance, (2) the date and amount of each of your purchases, (3) a description of each item you have charged, (4) a listing of all credits for returns, (5) any adjustments, and (6) the amount of the finance charge.

Along with the credit card has come the bane of most Americans: the computer. How many of us have been hit with charges by a faulty computer? How many of us have telephoned the company only to be greeted by another machine, which in turn advises the computer of our discontent? How many times have we been told that the problem will be corrected; yet the computer continues to spew out wrong information, and then, when we are finally exhausted, we get a lawyer's letter to the effect that we are being sued? Naturally it's for either a transaction we didn't make or for one that we had already paid.

What do you do with a computer besides pulling out the plug? Some people, of course, play along. One man in Richboro, Pennsylvania, was billed by an oil company for gasoline purchases in the amount of zero dollars and zero cents. That's right, the statement showed a balance of $0.00. He refused to pay this outstanding balance and the matter went into the hands of a collection agency. Another computer picked it up and carried it even further, to the point of a lawsuit, when finally the lawyer's secretary cried, "Hold it!" Needless to say, the matter *was* resolved.

If you're going after the computer, keep one thing in mind: It is the person who feeds the information into it that is the one you must get to. If, after sending letters of complaint, or even telephoning, you still get nowhere, then do what Groucho Marx once advised: "When you want something done, go right to the top." Send the next letter to the company president. That usually does the trick.

Under new federal legislation all lenders are required to acknowledge customers' written inquiries on billing errors within thirty days and to resolve them within sixty days. Until there is a resolution, you are *not* required to pay any service charges. During this period the lender is barred from taking action to collect the account or even from reporting it as delinquent to a credit bureau. The need for a lawyer here? None at all.

What if you sign a contract to buy goods or services and then change your mind? Suppose, for example, you're involved in a home-improvement transaction. The Truth-in-Lending Act calls for a three-day "cooling off" period, during which you can cancel the deal without any obligation. The creditor must furnish you with a standard "Notice of Right of Rescission." You must send this, or your cancellation notice, to the creditor by midnight of the third business day following the day on which you signed the contract. There is no penalty, fee, or charge, and you certainly don't need a lawyer to do this. Any down payment that you made must be promptly refunded.

What about door-to-door sales? Generally, a door-to-door salesperson is required to advise you of your right to cancel the sale and to give you a notice-of-cancellation card, provided the amount of the purchase is $25 or more. Thus you may cancel the transaction by mailing the cancellation card no later than midnight of the third business day following the day you sign any purchase agreement. If you misplace the card, you can send a letter expressing your intent to cancel. However, the three-day limit does not apply if the salesperson has not told you of your right to cancel, has not given you a card, or has not given you a copy of the signed purchase agreement. In those cases you can cancel the purchase at any time. (This right only applies to installment purchases.) Then, within ten days of your cancellation, the seller must refund all money you paid and return any trade-in items. You must hold the goods at your home for twenty days after your cancellation. The seller can either pick them up or ask you to ship them back at his expense. After twenty days, though, the goods are yours to keep, *and* you are still entitled to the refund. If the seller does not give you a refund within the ten-day period, you may begin a lawsuit to recover all payments, plus a $100 penalty and reasonable attorneys' fees.

What if the goods you bought are defective and you already paid for them through a retail-installment contract? You then have a right to withhold payment (which will prevent repossession) until the problem is solved.

By the way, if the creditor is after goods, not money, you should understand this: If you resist a creditor's request for repossession of your goods (such as your car), the creditor may go to court. In this event you would be wise to see an attorney who can advise you of your rights and help you in any defense. If the creditor does repossess your goods, you will be given notice as to the sale, and then you will have the chance to redeem those goods by paying off the debt beforehand. If any balance remains unpaid after repossession and sale, the creditor may bring a lawsuit against you to recover whatever money is still owed. Again, you should seek the services of an attorney in this instance.

YOU AND THE CREDIT BUREAU

Financial and personal data are stored in computer banks, and the data pass freely among credit bureaus. A credit report contains the history of an individual's use of credit, compiled from banks, finance companies, businessess. The reports, prepared and kept by credit bureaus, are to help businesses and lending institutions decide to give or deny credit.

An unfavorable credit report can mean more than the denial of credit cards or other services. It could involve the loss of a mortgage or insurance policy, or even a job. As a result of abuses on credit reporting, Congress passed the Fair Credit Reporting Act in 1971, and similar laws have been enacted by the states. These laws allow the individual to question a prospective lender as to the reasons why he has been turned down for credit.

So, if you learn that you have been denied credit—or even employment—because of an unfavorable credit rating, then you have a right to go to the credit bureau that supplied the rating. Somebody there must tell you the nature and substance of the report. If you find that the report contains false, incomplete, or obsolete data, you can challenge its accuracy. You don't need a lawyer to do this.

Upon giving proper notice to the credit bureau, the bureau must recheck the information within a reasonable period of time, usually about ten days. If the bureau finds that its information is indeed false, it must correct its report. Any information more than seven years old is generally deemed obsolete, but there are exceptions. If you are unable to prove that the negative information is false, you may enter your version, and the credit bureau must include that in all future reports. The bureau must send copies of your statement to anyone who has had access to its information during the previous six months, if you so request. If material was used for prospective employment, it must be sent to anyone who had access to it during the previous two years.

The Fair Credit Act does not require that the credit bureau give you the source of its information on your character or reputation. But failure of the credit bureau to follow the law in accordance with the Fair Credit Act can result in action by various agencies of the city, state, or federal government.

The federal government can also help when creditors attempt to dun you for bills that have been unjustly charged. The Federal Communications Commission (FCC), for example, forbids persons from using the telephone to frighten, torment, or harass. For example, if a credit company calls and threatens to take away your pet unless you pay up immediately, you can complain to the FCC in Washington or to any local branch office.

The Truth-in-Lending Act puts a limit on the amount of wages that can be garnished by a creditor. A *garnishment* is a notice ordering a person not to dispose of another's property or money in his possession pending settlement of a lawsuit. The amount cannot be more than 25 percent of a paycheck. In those states where the garnishment laws provide the employee with greater protection than the federal law, the state law governs.

It also prohibits an employer from firing an employee because his wages have been garnished. (Also, it prohibits the underworld from threatening you because you haven't paid!) In addition, it forbids a company to give away unsolicited credit cards, and it limits the consumer for charges arising out of the loss, theft, or misuse of his credit card to $50. Some states have even stricter regulations regarding a lost or stolen credit card. And keep in mind that the liability limit applies to *each* card you have.

TO COMPLAIN

If an item you bought is defective, here are the progressive steps you should follow:

1. Go back to the person who sold you the product.

2. Write or telephone the customer-relations department of the manufacturer with your complaint.

3. Write to the company's president. You can find his name in *Poor's Register of Corporations, Directors and Executives* or *Moody's Industrial Manual* in your local library. If these directories are not available in your local library, ask for the "directory" issues of such magazines as *Fortune, Business Week,* or *Forbes.*

4. Send copies of your letter to your local consumer-protection organization and organizations such as the Office of Consumer Affairs in Washington, Consumers Union, and your local Better Business Bureau.

5. Tell your problem to your local newspaper, TV, or radio station. That should do the trick. (However, make sure that what you tell them is the truth. If a newspaper prints something that is untrue and injures one's reputation, the paper and you may be open to an action for libel.)

Of course, you haven't exhausted all avenues. You can also contact the appropriate government agency. And don't forget about your representatives. Write to them, both in Washington and in your state legislature:

Senators: The Honorable _____
              Senate Office Building
              Washington, D.C. 20510

Representatives: The Honorable _____
              House Office Building
              Washington, D.C. 20515

And then if all else fails, take the matter into Small Claims Court. (See Chapter 9.)

PRODUCT LIABILITY

This is an area that is becoming extremely important. The public is considerably more aware of its rights and is taking action when an injury is incurred. In fact, the concept of strict liability is the prevailing doctrine today.

A recent case involved a thirteen-year-old boy who was burned over ninety percent of his body when the fuel tank of the car in which he was riding exploded after being hit from behind by a second car. The parents, on behalf of the youngster, sued the automobile company for negligence, claiming that the fuel tank was constructed in such a way that it would explode on even moderate impact. The jury awarded $2,841,000 for the injury, *plus* $125,000,000 in punitive damages. This became the highest product-injury award ever granted. (The court later reduced the $125-million figure to $3.5 million; the auto company is now appealing.)

If you are the victim of an injury from a defective product, you will have to prove that (1) the injury was caused by the product, and (2) that the product was defective. However, product liability is even more complicated. Because consumer products have become highly sophisticated and complex, the type of legal action that can be instituted against a manufacturer varies. Added to the confusion is the fact that the laws may differ from state to state. Thus it is strongly suggested that the services of an attorney be retained in cases involving product liability, especially when serious injury has occurred. If the potential award is large, a lawyer will usually take the case on a contingent arrangement, which means he will receive a part of the settlement as his fee, generally one-third. The contingent-fee arrangement (see Chapter 10) makes it financially easier for you to sue because you pay the lawyer nothing if you lose. Of course, you get nothing.

TO SUMMARIZE

In the consumer-conscious environment in which we now live, there are many state and local regulatory agencies that can come to the assistance of a disgruntled consumer, and rarely is a lawyer necessary. The fact is that it is the *exception* rather than the rule that it is necessary to obtain the services of an attorney in order for a consumer to seek relief in areas where he may have been wronged.

2

Human Rights

Not too long ago women were not allowed to smoke cigarettes in public. That archaic law, along with many similar ones, has vanished. Today, both federal and state laws cover just about every aspect of your rights, ranging from minimum wages to on-the-job safety, from equal opportunities to child labor laws, and even to women smoking in public. Usually these laws work, but like anything else in our society, you must stand guard against a violation of your rights. If those rights are infringed upon, you should know what to do, and that means whether or not to consult a lawyer.

The American Bar Association survey showed that for every 1,000 adults, 80 have a problem involving infringement of Constitutional rights, 60 have difficulty collecting their pay, and 90 are concerned with job discrimination.

To understand what to do when certain rights are infringed upon, you must understand what those rights are.

YOUR BASIC RIGHTS

Each individual is accorded basic fundamental rights by virtue of being a U.S. citizen, and these rights are insured under the Constitution. However, it is not the intention of this chapter to give you a course in

Constitutional law but merely to indicate what personal rights you have, what you can and cannot do with them, and, most importantly, what you can do if those rights are violated.

First, you have the right of freedom of speech, but this right is not absolute. It does not mean, for example, that you can use it in a crowded theater by yelling "fire" if there is no fire. In other words, each liberty has inherent in it a certain responsibility.

You have the right of freedom of assembly, which means that you can get together with any number of other persons to discuss the various problems and issues of the day, provided you are not interfering with the rights of others or endangering the safety of others.

You have the right of freedom of religion. As Americans—or in fact anyone living in this country—you have the right to select any religion and worship in your own style.

You have the right to vote. We have all recognized the series of events relating to the right to vote—from women to blacks, from twenty-one-year-olds to eighteen-year-olds. Fortunately, many of those discriminatory laws have been changed or ruled unconstitutional, and today the right to vote is relatively free of any sort of encumbrances.

You have the right to hold public office. However, any U.S. citizen who has been convicted of a felony cannot hold a federal public office. There are also some age restrictions. For example, you can't be under thirty-five to be President.

You have the right to keep and bear arms. This section of the law is often misconstrued. You cannot keep or bear arms, for instance, if it is contrary to specific laws in your state. You may have the right to keep a hunting rifle at home, but this doesn't necessarily mean you can have a howitzer in your basement.

You have the right to full enjoyment of your property. This means that no person, state, or government can take your property without what is known as *due process of law*, which means "by orderly procession of the law." Accordingly, the government cannot take your property or violate your rights under the Constitution without taking the necessary legal steps as proscribed by law.

You have the right to equal protection under the law. This is very much in evidence today where the civil rights of various members of the community have not been upheld. The courts have taken the offending parties—even governments—to task on discriminatory counts.

You have the right of due process of law. If you are arrested, you must be informed of your rights and given an opportunity to call a lawyer, family, or friend. It also means that you have a right to an attorney and to know what charges are being made against you. Suppose you are accused of violating a specific law? You have the right to challenge that law if it does not set up definite and ascertainable standards of guilt. For example, one fabled law, which provided that any person convicted of disorderly conduct at least three times was considered a gangster and subject to imprisonment, became invalid because it violated the requirements of due process.

You have the right of protection against self-incrimination. This means that you cannot be forced to testify against yourself. To understand this you need only refer to the various televised hearings before the committees of the Senate where the privilege has been invoked many times.

You have the right to *habeas corpus*, which means "delivering the body." If you have been arrested, you cannot be held beyond the time allotted under the law; or if you have been arrested on evidence illegally obtained, you may be released by means of a document called a *writ of habeas corpus*. In effect, this right safeguards you against illegal detention or imprisonment. The time differentials vary. In some states, twenty-four hours is considered a reasonable detainment period, while in other states you can be imprisoned for three days.

At the same time, you have the right against double jeopardy, in that you cannot be tried twice for the same crime.

If you ever go to trial, remember that you have the right to have your case heard before a jury.

You have the right to individual privacy. This right does not permit unreasonable search and seizure of your person or your property. Everyone is protected against the unreasonable search of his person and his property, including the seizure of his papers and personal belongings. A search and subsequent seizure is valid only if it is authorized by a warrant that is duly issued, or if the search and seizure are incidental to a valid arrest.

You have the right not to be assaulted. The difference between assault and battery is that battery requires actual physical contact, while an assault is mainly in the mind of the victim, e.g., a violent verbal attack or a threat of physical harm.

As long as we're talking about some forms of mental cruelty, let's take a look at the area of invasion of privacy and defamation.

DEFAMATION

Defamation usually occurs to a limited number of individuals, normally to public figures. Defamation is unjustly maligning the reputation of an individual. It primarily takes two forms: through the spoken word or through the written word. A verbal defamation that affects the reputation of an individual is *slander*. Defamation in writing is *libel*. For example, if somebody calls you a prostitute or a Communist (whether verbally or in writing), and you are neither, you have been defamed.

What do you do? There is not much you can or should do yourself. The first order of business is to hire the services of a competent attorney to protect your rights. The protection of those rights may be in the form of an injunction preventing the person who called you a Communist-prostitute from continuing to do so. Money damages to recompense you for the injury you have received is another form of relief. Both actions involve an area of the law that is very complex and should not be undertaken without professional guidance. Why?

The Supreme Court has determined that individual states should have the discretion to determine the standard of liability for defamation where a private individual is involved in a matter of public interest. However, where such a matter of public interest is involved, a public figure will have to show an actual, reckless disregard for the truth in order to recover damages, while a private individual will only have to show negligence. If a private person is defamed on a matter not of public interest, there is no requirement to show intention to defame. Recovering damages in such a case is allowed on the basis of the defamation alone, and reckless disregard for the truth is only relevant in fixing the extra damages, or punitive damages. Obviously an attorney is needed in this complex area of the law.

INVASION OF PRIVACY

Invasion of privacy is the violation of one's right to be left alone. It relates to the situation where the name or picture of an individual is used for purposes of trade or advertising, and it is a recent concept in the United States. (By recent we mean the last one hundred years.)

Today, only a few states have a right-of-privacy statute; others have what is known as court-enforced regulations, otherwise known as Rule of the Court, which prohibits using any material that may "shock one's sensibilities." An example is where an individual's name or likeness is used without permission in connection with the sale of some product or service. If you haven't given your permission in writing (or in some states, it can be oral), your only recourse may be through a lawsuit to prevent further use of your name or likeness and to seek money damages against the offending parties. Clearly this requires specific expertise, and the services of an attorney should be obtained.

Incidentally, the press is not automatically immune from an invasion-of-privacy action just because of freedom of the press. A case in Alabama not too long ago involved a newspaper that had shown a picture of a lady with her dress blown up by air jets in a funhouse at a country fair. The publisher said that this was of legitimate news value. The court felt differently and decided against the publisher. The reason? The picture was *not* of legitimate news value since there was nothing in it to which the public was entitled to be informed.

What happens when it's not a newspaper or other entity that invades your privacy? What happens if it's the government?

Congress has determined that the privacy of an individual is directly affected by the collection, maintenance, use, and dissemination of information by federal agents. How many of your individual freedoms are altered by the FBI having a dossier on you? Furthermore, the increasing use of computers and sophisticated information technology, although essential to the operation of the government, greatly magnifies the potential for harming an individual's privacy. Therefore Congress, recognizing and protecting the right to privacy, has deemed it necessary and proper to regulate the collection, maintenance, use, and dissemination of information by such agencies.

Accordingly, the Right of Privacy Law was enacted in order to provide certain protections for an individual against an invasion of his personal rights by requiring those agencies to permit an individual to decide what records of his can be used. This law also prevents those records from being made available for any other purpose without the individual's consent.

It also permits an individual to gain access to his records in federal agencies so that he can correct such records. Thus a law was enacted to assure that a collection of information could only be for lawful purposes, but that any violation of a citizen's rights under the statute would subject the government to a civil suit for damages. It goes without saying that suing the government is best left in the hands of a competent attorney.

How do you find out about these records? The National Archives of the United States publishes a federal register of those agencies that might be involved in the collection and dissemination of information concerning you as a citizen. The register *is* available to you. (See the Appendix.) Once you have obtained the register, you can make inquiries directly to those agencies, either in person or by mail. For example, suppose you had been in the United States Marine Corps and wanted to find out about your military service record: the results of your tests, your conduct, your awards. By following the instructions in the front of the book, you will be able to locate a section entitled "Marine Corps Military Personnel Records" under the Department of Defense. This section will tell you how to obtain a copy of your own personnel record.

The procedure to follow is simple: Give your full name and address. Specify the system of record you believe contains information about you. Provide the relevant facts as outlined in the digest section of the register. For instance, if you are inquiring about any contact you may have had with the government, such as a loan application, a contract, or a grant application, give the data and subject matter of that contact, plus any identifying numbers from documents you may have previously received.

It is helpful to include the words "Privacy Act Request" on the front of your envelope. The agency may require some proof of your identity, such as another legal document with your full name and address, or a document that has your signature and photograph (a passport or an employment insurance book will do). A fee may be charged for a copy of those records.

EQUAL OPPORTUNITIES

A major concern for most people is the area of equal rights, and it encompasses everything from discrimination in employment to discrimination in housing.

Employment

The equal-protection clause of the Fourteenth Amendment to the Constitution specifically prohibits discrimination by federal, state, or local governments against any category of citizens involved in any government-related activity.

In 1870 a civil rights act provided that all Americans would have the same right as "white citizens to enter into contracts." Thus, if you weren't white, you had the right to sue in federal or state court if you were the victim of job discrimination because of your race. In fact, today, unions cannot be granted governmental support if they practice discrimination. Moreover, companies cannot receive government contracts if they practice job discrimination.

In 1964 another civil rights act was passed specifically banning job discrimination in private employment because of race, sex, religion, or national origin. This act also prohibits discrimination against anyone who wants to join a union or who seeks the services of an employment agency, and it also applies to help-wanted ads, pay scales, promotions, pension plans, and other fringe benefits. This applies to all employers with fifteen or more employees, and to employees of the state and local government and educational facilities.

In addition, a number of states now have laws outlawing discrimination in hiring and in the amount of money one can be paid. These laws affect not only the people who employ you but also agencies and unions who are involved in particular areas. In most states these laws come under the heading "Fair Employment Practices Act."

But it gets even broader. Legislation known as the 1967 Age Discrimination in Employment Act prohibits employers from firing or discriminating against employees in certain age brackets. For example, the act bans the firing or the refusal to hire persons forty to sixty-five because of that age alone. Of course there are certain conditions here. It generally applies to employers having twenty or more workers, and it doesn't cover certain age qualifications. If you are a thirty-year-old actress, and a theatrical producer is looking for someone to play the part of a five-year-old, there is not much you can do. That isn't age discrimination. The act also forbids employment agencies from refusing to refer an applicant for a job because of the applicant's age; in fact, ads specifying certain age requirements by employers in help-wanted ads are now prohibited.

As a result, the Equal Employment Opportunity Commission (EOC) has been established to investigate complaints against businesses involved in interstate commerce with more than twenty-five employees. Therefore, if you feel that you have been discriminated against because of your age, a complaint could be made to the EOC or to the Department of Labor in your state. (The EOC also handles complaints relating to discrimination because of color or national origin.) The EOC will investigate the charges and in many instances will insure the employment of an employee if he has, in fact, been discriminated against.

Today, the only grounds for job discrimination on the basis of sex are if (1) sex is a "bona fide occupational qualification," such as in modeling, or (2) if hiring a woman would violate certain moral codes. Accordingly, women must be considered for jobs they usually didn't apply for in the past: dock work, trucking, parcel-post deliveries. They must also be considered for jobs as "salespeople," and a company must admit qualified women to their executive training programs under the same conditions as men.

Of course, the biggest problem has been money. The Census Bureau reports that as of 1975 American women were earning 60 percent of what men earned. There is no question that even when men and women hold similar jobs the pay they get is usually unequal, and in some occupations this gap is much wider than the 60-percent average.

In 1964 the Equal Pay Act went into effect, administered by the Wage and Hour Division, Employment Standards Administration, U.S. Department of Labor. Write to them with your complaint, and they'll look into it.

Of course, with the advent of the proposed Equal Rights Amendment, great focus has been placed on discrimination in employment with respect to women. And there is no doubt that there has been discrimination. In fact, as recently as 1966, three states prohibited women from serving on a jury. (This practice was ultimately declared unconstitutional by the Supreme Court.)

In addition to contacting various governmental agencies to report discrimination (this does not require the services of an attorney), private lawsuits have been filed by women throughout the country against organizations or employees who have practiced sex discrimination, both in employment and promotion practices. These lawsuits do require the services of an attorney. Fortunately most of these cases have been decided in behalf of the woman.

Another area where human rights are increasingly being defended is that of "Gay Rights." This is currently an extremely volatile subject. As of this writing, at least thirty-seven municipalities have homosexual-rights ordinances, protecting those individuals in employment and in other areas.

In New York City the mayor has issued an executive order forbidding discrimination against homosexuals in municipal government. Two other New York localities, Ithaca and Alfred, have taken similar action. In San Francisco the Board of Supervisors, in March 1978, approved a homosexual-rights ordinance that many consider the most stringent in the nation. That ordinance bans discrimination in employment, housing, and public accommodations based on sexual preference.

However, in April 1978 voters in St. Paul, Minnesota, repealed a four-year-old city ordinance prohibiting discrimination on the basis of "affectional or sexual preference." Supporters of the repeal spoke of morality and protecting children from homosexual teachers, while opponents put the question in the context of human rights.

Most recently (in November, 1978), California voters, in the nation's first statewide vote on homosexual rights, refused to accept a proposal that would have banned hiring homosexual teachers in the public school system. In Seattle, an effort to repeal a homosexual rights law was also beaten.

Although the situation is controversial, the fact remains that if legislation against such discrimination exists in your locality, and there has been discrimination, by all means contact the appropriate agency in your town and *demand* that action be taken.

Housing

The 1968 Civil Rights Act, known as the "fair housing" statute, specifically guarantees equal access to housing and prohibits discrimination on the basis of color, race, religion, or national origin.

If you are a member of a minority group and you have been discriminated against in buying or renting a house (or apartment), you can take action.

File a complaint with the Secretary of Housing and Urban Development, Washington, D.C. 20410, to the attention of Fair Housing, or file a lawsuit with the United States District Court. The first route doesn't need a lawyer; the second one does. You can do both.

Credit

The 1974 Equal Credit Opportunity Act, an amendment to the Truth-in-Lending Act (discussed in Chapter 1), makes it illegal for a bank or any other lender to deny you credit on the basis of sex or marital status. The same agencies that enforce the Truth-in-Lending Act enforce this law.

Never before has there been such recognition of the rights of individuals in this country as there is now. In the areas of employment, schools, and housing regulatory agencies and commissions are available and receptive to the needs of the citizens. However, one of your best tools is still your telephone book. If, for example, you are seeking housing in a local area and cannot obtain it because of "something" about your race, color, or creed, check those agencies involved in the area of human rights. Make the proper inquiry and your complaint will be heard. You can of course do this without the need to hire an attorney. It is simply a question of finding out which agency is involved.

(See the Appendix for a listing of the agencies and organizations to which you should write if you feel your rights have been violated or you have been discriminated against in any of these areas.)

CHANGING YOUR NAME

Any individual in the United States has a right to change the name he or she was born with. Clearly, there are times where the name a person was given at birth could be embarrassing later on. And some names, because of their spelling, are just too difficult to pronounce. As a result, the laws permit an individual to change his name so long as the purpose of the change is not to avoid creditors or to commit fraud. The process is readily available to all, and you merely have to contact the clerk of the court in your jurisdiction for the rules.

Generally, an affidavit stating the reason for the change is signed by the individual. Once that affidavit (and whatever filing fee is necessary) is filed with the court, it may be necessary to publish your intention in two newspapers. However, check the laws of your state.

Are the services of an attorney required? If you follow the rules of the court, legal counsel isn't necessary. (See the Appendix for a sample affidavit form, but note that this may not be applicable in your jurisdiction.)

TO SUMMARIZE

The easiest route to solving most of the problems regarding your rights is to check your phone book for a listing of the agencies involved in your particular area of concern. Make a complaint either in writing or in person, and the agency will investigate the problem. You don't need a lawyer to do this. Any matters requiring the institution of legal action by you would, of course, be best served by obtaining legal counsel.

3

Family Matters

It is only when the possibility of separation and divorce arises that most people will consider an attorney necessary to handle family matters. There are, however, other occasions when you may need legal advice: for a prenuptial contract, for adoption proceedings, if your child damages a neighbor's property. We will consider these and related problems in this chapter to determine when an attorney's services are needed.

MARRIAGE

You have to obtain a license to be married, but some states also require a waiting period, certain age requirements, or a blood test. In Alabama a male under the age of twenty-one needs parental consent to get married, whereas for a female, the age limit is eighteen. In Florida, however, a female must be twenty-one to avoid parental consent, while a female in Hawaii must be at least sixteen. Your local marriage-license bureau can tell you the age requirements. They'll also tell you if a blood test is necessary. The test is given primarily to make sure that a social disease has not been contracted by one (or both) of the parties to the marriage. In Kentucky a blood test is required to obtain a license, whereas Maryland has no requirement. And don't forget the waiting period. Maryland has a two-day layoff to cool your heels before you can apply for a license, while

Louisiana has no waiting period. It is mandatory that you check the laws of your state as to the requirements for obtaining a marriage license. Again, there is no big deal about this. Simply call the clerk of the court in your city or county, or call the marriage bureau, for all the information you need. You don't need a lawyer to do any of this.

If you don't want a formalized arrangement, you might want to find out whether your state approves of common-law marriages. Common-law marriage means a couple lives together and presents themselves to the public as man and wife, although they were never actually married by a judge, member of the clergy, or other official. It is less common today, but some states still recognize this concept. Remember, you are simply interested in answers to these questions: Who may marry? At what age may they marry? How can it be done? Who can perform the ceremony? Don't minimize any of this. Suppose you want to marry your first cousin. Some states, for example, won't even permit a woman to marry her brother-in-law.

One law you needn't bother to check concerns interracial marriages, which are now perfectly permissible. The previous laws preventing such marriages have been declared unconstitutional by the Supreme Court. In a landmark decision (1967), the court said that no state could enforce a law arbitrarily restricting the basic freedom of any citizen or group of citizens, and this included the "freedom to marry."

All of this presupposes that everything is running smoothly. What happens, though, if there is a proposal to marry and one party pulls out of the deal? Generally an offer to marry and its acceptance are recognized by the law as a binding contract. Accordingly, if a man and woman agree to end their engagement, the contract is deemed automatically terminated. However, you can't take this as gospel in *all* jurisdictions. For instance, in a few states damage suits may be brought against third parties who have been instrumental in breaking up an engagement. This means that a man may demand money damages from another man who stole his fiancé by offering her greater comforts than he could provide. By the same token, some states recognize the validity of a lawsuit where a woman sues her rival who had lured her "intended" away through sexual seduction.

Because there are so many variables when it comes to broken engagements, it would be foolhardy to try to institute any legal action without knowing the law. A common example: the question of whether one has a legal right to recover engagement or wedding gifts. This has been decided differently by different courts. An engagement ring is considered a pledge for the contract of marriage. The general rule has been that if the man breaches the pledge, the woman can keep the ring Of course, if she calls off the wedding, the ring should be returned.

In the majority of the cases engagement rings have been ordered by the court to be returned to the donor. However, it's not always so dogmatic. You have to consider what legal action is available to you based on your local law. In a New York case, a separated but not yet divorced man sued his "fiancé" for the return of a $50,000 ring. The term "fiancé" is used loosely because he gave her the ring on the condition that *as soon as he was divorced* she would marry him. After a long wait she backed out, and consequently he instituted suit for return of the ring.

The court ruled that she could keep the gem. Why? It reasoned that the man was still married, and therefore it was against the public policy (meaning against the public good) of that state to enforce an arrangement that was contingent on a divorce. Accordingly, that condition was deemed removed from the gift, and the woman retained the ring.

A lawyer here? With $50,000 riding on the outcome, the answer is obvious. However, you should be practical. Certainly it wouldn't make much sense to spend $100 in legal fees to try to get back a ring worth $19.98.

One specific area of marriage that a number of people today are considering involves the antenuptial or premarital agreement, which is simply a written document that sets forth the obligations and responsibilities of the parties to the marriage and, most importantly, the division of their property. This type of agreement is used primarily in the eight community-property states: Arizona, California, Idaho, Louisiana, Nevada, New Mexico, Texas, and Washington. In these states earnings of the husband and wife are legally considered to be merged; that is, they are common property. The use of this agreement separates the property of the couple.

The antenuptial agreement is also frequently employed in second marriages where both parties have children by their first partners and want certain mutual protections, the intention being that neither partner would inherit the other's estate. It is also used by some of the affluent. For example, the marriage of Aristotle Onassis and Jacqueline Kennedy was purportedly memorialized by a premarital contract: who sleeps where, how much allowance is one party to receive, who gets what if the marriage doesn't last, and other assorted provisions.

Is a lawyer necessary here? Most definitely. Because of the intricacies of such an agreement, it is best to have a lawyer draw up the document. After all, you want to make sure certain aspects of the law are properly covered. Did you know, for instance, that husbands and wives can sue each other in order to establish property rights or even to press claims from business transactions between them? But, it's true that only a few states will permit lawsuits by one spouse against the other with respect to personal injury and property damage. A distinction is made here between rights and damages, and it should be considered. Therefore it is extremely important that the document reflects the law of your jurisdiction in clear and precise terms.

To be sure, there are probably those who for no other reason than wanting to be careful (or perhaps for more secretive reasons) decide that it would be beneficial to have a premarital contract spelling out the rights and obligations of both parties. If this is the case, you should obtain proper legal guidance so that the agreement you do sign is valid under the laws of your state and protects what you want protected.

As far as costs are concerned, much will depend on how involved the agreement is. Legal fees may range from $100 up to draw such an agreement.

CHILDREN

There is rarely a need for your friendly counselor with regard to children. The bulk of your money will go toward the obstetrician, the hospital, and diapers. The question parents frequently ask concerns the liability for wrongs done by the child. For example, if your four-year-old chucks a baseball through your next-door neighbor's picture window, who's liable? The law generally provides that if a child is of such tender years as to lack the experience that would enable him to realize the presence of danger or the results of his actions, he cannot be sued.

By the same token, you as the parent may not be liable either if you had no knowledge of or didn't contribute to the wrongdoing. For the most part, without knowledge, a parent is not liable, but recently a number of states have been exploring the possibility of making the parents responsible to innocent third parties for the wrongs committed by their children. Thus, if a serious situation has been created by your child, the services of a lawyer should be retained in order to explain the rights and obligations under the laws of your state.

ADOPTIONS

To adopt, according to Webster, is to "take into one's own family by *legal process* and treat as one's own child." Note the italicized words.

One out of four women has trouble conceiving a child, and accordingly the demand for children is greater than the supply. So, the question of adoption warrants serious consideration.

Basically the procedure involves petitioning a court by those seeking the adoption, with the express consent of the natural parents. The requirements in each state may differ, and the determination of when you may need a lawyer often turns on the kind of adoption.

One avenue to adoption is through state agencies. You can simply go to a state or city adoption agency. The agency places the child and handles all the technicalities involved, including the legal ones. You can always bring in your own attorney, but the agency generally has staff attorneys, and the fees are low.

Most people have the agency take care of all aspects of the adoption. It's a rather simple procedure in most states with a minimum of fuss and cost. Again, there is little need to have an outside lawyer because the agency provides one. Adoptions through state agencies do not involve any other state; it's primarily an intrastate arrangement.

The exception to this concerns the private adoption route, particularly when two states are involved. For example, take the couple from New York. The wife couldn't have children, so they tried to adopt through a state agency. At the time, though, the demand was far greater than the supply, and they were put on a lengthy waiting list. However, the husband had a pediatrician friend in Baltimore. He in turn contacted an obstetrician, and soon thereafter the couple was told of a pregnant but unmarried woman who would be delivering in five months. She wanted to put the child up for adoption.

Now, was it necessary to have lawyers at this point? Could the couple have arranged the adoption on their own? The answer is based on the following information:

The law in Maryland required that (1) a certain number of court appearances by the pregnant woman was necessary, (2) a specific "formality" had to be carried out at the hospital, and (3) a number of papers had to be filed after the baby was born. This meant that the couple would have to travel 250 miles to appear in court. They also would have to carry out the requirements of the law of that state while undergoing the emotional experience of adoption. The couple decided to turn the matter over to counsel. They immediately contacted an attorney on Long Island who was knowledgeable in adoption proceedings, and he referred the matter to a correspondent attorney in Baltimore.

It was the wisest thing they could have done, because Maryland specified the ways in which the child could be adopted. New York had nothing to say about it, at least not at this point. The Baltimore lawyer had to obtain the written consent of the pregnant woman at various intervals over the five-month period prior to delivery. In effect, it was a constant reaffirmation process. In addition, certain documents had to be filed with the court at specific times. When the baby was born and the couple was told to come to the hospital the next day to receive the child, they were instructed to bring with them three certified checks for payment: to the hospital, the doctor, and the lawyer. Everything had to be in accordance with Maryland law.

But the next step was perhaps the most heartrending of all. Maryland had a law as to the manner in which the child was to be turned over to the new parents. The husband told the story:

> I watched a small, blonde-haired girl emerge from behind the hospital's sliding glass doors. She looked no more than sixteen, thinnish, with metal-rimmed glasses and a clear, almost bland face. I walked with my wife toward the girl, who was then accompanied by a nurse and our lawyer. They stood on the hospital steps. When the nurse saw us approaching, she left and the two people remaining looked at each other encouragingly. Then their eyes dropped to a bundle wrapped in a soft, yellow blanket that the girl cradled in her arms.
>
> As soon as we reached them, the lawyer began the introductions. He turned to the girl. "Would you like to give the baby to . . . ?" She nodded, and the two mothers stepped toward each other. I guess you could say it was the one who carried the baby physically and the one who had carried it emotionally.
>
> They stared at each other for the longest time. Then, my wife leaned forward so that the girl could do nothing but hold her arms out too, and each held a portion of the yellow blanket. I could hear someone whispering, "Thank you very much. Thank you." But all I could see were tears flowing down the cheeks of both mothers through a damp cloud of my own. God, even the lawyer had to look away. I'll never forget that moment. Never.

It still was not over. The couple then returned to New York and waited, because New York law required a six-month probationary period before the adoption could become final. Technically that meant it was still possible to lose the child if the natural mother changed her mind. Fortunately, the six-month period came and went, and the couple filed for a final order of adoption in family court. It was granted, and the ordeal was over.

The cost? Considering what was involved, it was rather minimal. The couple paid $850 to the lawyer in Baltimore, $600 to the hospital, and $350 to the doctor, plus another $350 to the New York lawyer.

Of course, there is also the "black market" route to adopting children. This involves buying and selling illegitimate children at extraordinary sums of money. A high, five-figure amount to obtain a child (usually from another state) is not unusual. The problem, though, is obvious. An adoption decree can be set aside at the court's discretion even years after it is issued, if there is evidence of fraud or misrepresentation. And the chances of finding deceit in "black market" trafficking of children is quite good. Accordingly, caution must be exercised.

Because adoption proceedings are so complicated, it is both impractical and unwise to attempt to go through them without legal counsel. This is especially true in private adoptions, where an attorney is mandatory in order to ascertain the legal status of the adopted child in your jurisdiction, prepare the necessary documents, and follow the matter from the adoption petition to the final court decree. In other words, the lawyer's job is to safeguard the interests of both the adopting parents and the adopted child.

SEPARATION AND DIVORCE

This is the heart of legal services with respect to the area in the law known as Domestic Relations. Here is where the number one concern regarding the use of lawyers comes into focus.

A marriage is a civil contract between a man and a woman, and the state has an interest in preserving it. Accordingly, a marriage can be dissolved *only* as provided by law.

It would be an understatement to say that divorce is on the upswing. In the United States one out of every three marriages ends in divorce, and that ratio is closing fast. The Census Bureau estimates that within three years, the $33^1/3$ percent will increase to a staggering 50 percent. In fact, in 1978 there were more than 1,700,000 divorces.

First, let's get some terms straight:

A *separation* does not end the marriage, although it certainly leads to it. You and your spouse decide to live apart. One of you moves out. However, neither of you is free to marry. In effect, although you are legally separated and can come and go as you please, you are still legally married.

A *divorce decree* says it all. Your marriage is finished.

An *annulment* is a court order saying, in effect that the marriage never took place. Generally, it results from a wedding that was entered into under duress or, even more common, where one party (usually the female) is under age.

A *void marriage* is one that is deemed illegal from the beginning, primarily because it violates well-known laws such as bigamy; accordingly, the second "marriage" is declared invalid.

A *voidable marriage* is a union that can be ended through certain proceedings. Ordinarily it applies in cases of fraud or where there is a misrepresentation by one party that causes the other to enter into a marriage. It also comes into play where a serious disease of one party is hidden from the other. The classic case is the husband-to-be who indicates prior to the marriage that he wants children and then does an about-face after the ceremony.

How do you and the lawyers fit into all this? It should be noted first that a lawyer's job is to (1) Explain the laws and your rights and obligations involved in dissolving the marital relationship, and (2) point out the consequences. The lawyer also defines the requirements. For example, certain jurisdictions enable you to bring an action for absolute divorce based on legal separation; others do not. In some states, such as Maine, you must be separated for one year in order to file for a divorce. And residency requirements differ. Massachusetts requires two years of residency, Arkansas three months, and Nevada six weeks. The bases for ending a marriage do vary confusingly from state to state. (The prerequisites are included in the Appendix.)

However, once you understand the ground rules, the key as to whether or not you need a lawyer may very well turn on the extent of the dispute between the parties.

Look at it this way: If there is no serious issue between you and your spouse concerning children and the division of property, there is a possibility for you to acquire your own divorce without the assistance of an attorney. *But,* you and your spouse must be able to divide the property without problems. This is called a *friendly divorce.*

Spouses can attempt to resolve their situation on the basis of (a) property division, (b) custodial rights of the child, and (c) payments by one spouse to the other. All of this can be formulated in a document commonly called a *separation agreement.*

To reiterate, a legal separation means living apart under a written agreement of separation. The separation agreement is a detailed contract that sets forth the rights and duties of both parties. Important factors must be considered when drawing up a separation agreement, however.

1. *Alimony:* How much is one spouse to pay the other? The original theory of alimony was to provide the wife with some kind of financial security. Of course, this presupposes that the man is making the payments, although that concept is changing.

How much do you pay and for how long? Payments usually continue for the length of time your ex remains unmarried. Naturally, when the ex dies, the payments automatically stop. As a guideline, money paid as alimony usually ranges between 25 and 65 percent of your income. One-third, however, is considered the norm. What you will pay depends on a number of factors, among which is the law in your state, your income, and your ex's income.

Who pays whom? A number of jurisdictions (Iowa, North Dakota) have enacted laws giving the divorce court power to grant alimony to a husband under a statute that provides that "either party may be required to pay the same." And laws in some states (Ohio, Oregon, North Dakota) now specifically authorize allowances of alimony to the ex-husband. In fact, the right of a husband to receive an award of permanent alimony under special statutes is recognized in California, Iowa, Massachusetts, North Dakota, Ohio, Oklahoma, Pennsylvania, and Washington.

2. *Child Support:* How much is one spouse to pay to the other for child support, and for how long a time? These payments continue until the child reaches the age of majority, marries, enters the military service, or does something else to indicate that he or she is no longer under your wing. The general law is that a parent is to support a child until that child is emancipated, usually at the age of eighteen.

The amount of money you pay depends on the kind of financial arrangement you have made. There is no specific minimum, and usually it is determined by the needs of the child and the ability of the parents to pay. One thing is certain, though: Child support is an extremely serious consideration, and the courts watch this area more than any other. Failure to maintain payments can result in the parents being brought up on contempt-of-court charges.

The court does have the right to modify separation agreements if it feels the child is not receiving the proper amount of money. This instance has been primarily where the husband has been paying the wife, but it has gone the other way too. In a recent case in New York, the state's highest court ruled unanimously that the former wife had to pay certain sums as child support to the former husband, who had retained custody of the child.

3. *Custody:* Who retains custody of the children? Most of the major battles are fought in this area. Three basic forms of custody are (1) where a child lives most of the year with one parent, but both parents jointly share in the upbringing: (2) where the child lives one-half of the time with one

parent and one-half with the other; and (3) where children are split up between the two parents; one goes with the mother, and the other goes with the father.

Courts oversee this carefully, for they have always taken a posture of judging what's in the "best interest" of the child. A prominent family relations attorney in Philadelphia, Harry Schwartz, says that "the courts in this city are beginning to wrestle more and more with the problem of which parent is better fit rather than which is unfit."

4. *Visitation Rights:* Visitation rights will depend on what form of custody has been agreed to.

5. *Bank Accounts, Stocks, and Bonds:* How are they to be divided? Who gets what?

6. *Personal and Real Property:* This is particularly important to those people residing in community-property states, where the husband and wife own everything jointly. This doesn't mean that if one person comes into a marriage owning certain property, the other person would automatically have a share of it. However, if the couple treat the property as part of their joint ownership, that property could be considered under the community-property law. For example, if a man owned a particular house prior to his marriage but afterward included the mortgage payments in the couple's joint income-tax return, then under the community property law that house would be considered the joint property of both parties.

Splitting up any kind of property is a sticky matter. For instance, a case pending in Colorado involves a Denver couple who are in litigation over tickets to the Broncos' games. The former husband claims that his former wife "forged" his signature on a letter to the Denver Broncos asking that his two season tickets be placed in her name. This, the man said, had caused him "extreme mental anguish."

After you have considered all of these points, you will know whether or not you are still talking about a "friendly" divorce. If not, then it is best to see a lawyer at once. Of course, if you've hurdled these obstacles, you are ready to consider the next aspect: the divorce itself.

Getting a divorce is easier than ever before, but it is still complicated by the laws in each various state. For example, residency requirements in your state may dictate that you live within those borders for a certain period of time. And there are different aspects of how the divorce can be effected.

The "Fault" Way

Traditionally a divorce action is a legal proceeding whereby one party sues the other, thereby saying in effect that one person is at fault and the other is free of guilt.

In a "fault" divorce it is necessary for the couple to establish the grounds for the dissolution of a marriage in their state. Almost all states will grant a divorce for adultery, but only three recognize attempted murder of a spouse as adequate grounds. One of these even goes so far as to define it as an attempt to take the life of a spouse "with poison or some other means showing malice." In New York, for example, there are six grounds: cruel and inhuman treatment, abandonment, confinement of one person in prison for the past three years, adultery, living apart for one or more years under a court order, and living apart for at least one year under a separation agreement duly filed with the court. (See the Appendix for the grounds of divorce in each state.)

As soon as the grounds are established, one party sues the other by the service of a summons (commencement of the action) and a complaint (the specification of the charges of the action). There is a hearing, sometimes an appearance at a Conciliation Board, and then a trial, at which point the court will sign the final divorce decree. (Incidentally, most lawyers recommend the parties agree that the terms and conditions of the separation agreement be part of the divorce decree. It makes life much simpler.)

Do you need a lawyer to do this? Generally if the divorce is a friendly one and there are few, if any, complications, the parties might be able to work it out themselves with the help of the clerks in the matrimonial courts. Naturally, whenever you are dealing with a lawsuit, it is always wise to seek competent legal assistance to make sure that all the proper steps are taken.

The "No-Fault" Way

More and more states are doing away with the principle of a lawsuit and, instead, are passing "no-fault" divorce laws. The procedure in a "no-fault" divorce does not rely on customary divorce grounds, such as the age-old one of adultery. Although these new statutes vary in their details, all of them make it unnecessary for one spouse to prove the other was at fault in order to get a divorce; in other words, no wrongdoing need be proved to dissolve the marriage. Instead, they recognize the right of the parties to terminate a dead marriage by mutual agreement. In effect, the intention is to reduce the bitterness that usually accompanies divorce proceedings.

The requirements for a no-fault divorce are relatively simple. Divorce has been replaced with a *Dissolution of Marriage*, granting that the marriage has broken down to the point where there is no reasonable likelihood that it can be restored.

A couple in California, each with independent careers and no children, decide to dissolve their marriage. Neither wants alimony, and there is little property to divide. Do they need a lawyer?

In a no-fault divorce state, if it is an uncontested, uncomplicated divorce based on irreconcilable differences, the parties can pretty much do it themselves. They can go to the courthouse and fill out certain forms. If necessary, they can call on the clerk for help. If it is after hours and the court is closed, they may be able to acquire these papers commercially from a local stationery store that stocks legal forms.

They file the papers and wait for a trial date to be assigned by the court, usually within thirty to sixty days. They appear in court on the date specified, answer certain questions, and the marriage is dissolved. It's quick, easy, and relatively painless, or as painless as divorce ever can be. The costs are minimal too.

Naturally, even in no-fault divorce states, if a serious problem arises, or if you are unsure of the requirements for a dissolution in your state, seek professional guidance.

The "Other" Way

Fast divorces have always been popular. These quickies usually take place outside the United States, and they can be accomplished in a number of ways. For instance, a recent advertisement in the New York *Times* stated: DIVORCE IN ONE MONTH. The reader was asked to contact a law firm in Belgium for free information. We did.

We received a two-page letter explaining that divorce applications were being processed through either the Dominican Republic or Haiti, the reason being that there was no residency requirement to speak of, and that these two countries were considerably more lenient about the grounds for divorce.

In answer to a self-asked question as to whether the divorces were valid here, the writer (who claimed to be a law professor) advised that all states have accepted such quick divorces "if properly presented to the court."

Apparently the terms of the divorce are worked out by the lawyers in Belgium and then processed through another lawyer in either of these two countries. The all-inclusive price of $1,850 covers the legal fee for the Belgian lawyer, the fee for the lawyer in either the Dominican Republic or Haiti, court costs, translations, authentication by a foreign embassy, issue of decree, and any other necessary papers.

Do you have to be present in court? According to the professor, in Haiti at least one party should be present, while in the Dominican Republic the divorce application is processed through a lawyer. However, certain aspects should be noted. This type of divorce can also be processed through American lawyers too—and probably for less money. So, there may be no reason for you to go through Belgium.

Also, you could do it yourself. All you have to do is contact the Dominican Republic or Haitian Embassy and request the requirements. You can then tie in your divorce with a vacation or perhaps obtain the dissolution of your marriage on the way back from a business trip.

You should be cautious about the validity of such a divorce decree in your state. The general rule of law is that if both you and your spouse agree to a foreign-secured divorce, it will probably be considered valid. However, if only one side consents, it may not be.

WARNING: We are not passing judgment on this method in any way. We are simply alerting you to its existence. It is then up to you to explore it further.

Now, where does the lawyer fit in regarding divorces in general?

Judith Malone Finch, a New York and California attorney, lives in San Diego, California, where she specializes in matrimonial law. We asked her whether marital problems were common only to urban centers.

"No. It's unimportant where you live. Living in a city or country doesn't necessarily affect matrimonial bliss. In other words, divorce actions are not dictated by the pressures of only city living."

Is there a pattern as to who seeks you out on domestic problems?

"It's usually someone who needs guidance. For example, the older woman. She always assumed that her financial future was secure. Now she is not so sure. She, more than anyone else, needs direction. In younger women, I find that security is not that big a factor. These women want out of a marriage with as little frustration as possible. In effect, they are looking to themselves for financial security."

Are the services of a lawyer necessary then?

"An older woman who has been a wife and mother and has been divorced from the business world desperately needs advice. She must have someone to give her sound tax information and financial planning. Such a woman without help is usually at the mercy of a more experienced husband."

Although two-thirds of her clients are women, Mrs. Finch feels many of her answers apply to men as well.

"For the working man or woman who is reasonably independent and who has his or her own profession and who can look after his or her own rights, self-representation makes a lot of sense."

Self-representation? Can it be done? It depends. There are books on the market about doing your own divorce. There are even do-it-yourself kits, especially in no-fault states like California, where the dissolution of a marriage is not as difficult to obtain as in other jurisdictions. In fact, even if it were not so simplistic, to many people the aggravation and confusion that can result from acting as your own lawyer is endurable when one considers lawyer's fees. For example, the fee range for an uncontested or friendly divorce might cost anywhere from $750 to $2,000, depending on your state and the specific procedures to be followed.

The do-it-yourself concept, which has recommended itself to the public by virtue of a combination of a rising inflation and a sinking dollar, has transcended the traditional image of simply fixing, building, or taking apart. People today are actually handling many of their own legal problems in areas where they are equipped to handle them.

Of course self-representation is not appropriate for every problem. But if it isn't, you still have access to help. Referral services at the bar associations permit a nonlawyer to visit with an attorney for a low fee. The cost is about $15. In fact, for about $50, some lawyers will help a couple fill out whatever forms are essential to satisfy legal requirements.

One blatant exception to self-representation in a divorce is, of course, children. Most lawyers interviewed draw the line when children are involved. If custody is an issue, they feel it is best to have the lawyer play a role somewhere in the settlement. And interestingly enough, statistics show that the most extensive use of a lawyer today is as a negotiator in a divorce action.

Therefore, the best advise is the lawyer's own. If lawyers are confused as to the procedure to follow, they will call the court for answers. The clerk of the court often has more answers about a specific legal procedure than lawyers themselves. Most clerks (in matrimonial courts especially) are extremely helpful. This might be your first step. Of course, it goes without saying that if you don't call the clerk, call a lawyer.

TO SUMMARIZE

Obviously you don't need a lawyer to get married unless you want a premarital contract.

With respect to adopting children, you most certainly need a lawyer for private adoptions, but not for state ones.

Divorce? Well, by now you should be able to determine whether you are able to do your own divorce or whether the services of legal counsel are necessary. The no-fault states have made it easier for self-representation, but, again, be careful. The do-it-yourself concept is only good if the dissolution is an uncomplicated one.

4

Real Property Transactions

Basic differences exist between renting and buying: On one hand, you own something; on the other, someone else owns it, and you are simply given license to use the premises.

RENTING

You rent an apartment, a house, a car, a lawnmower—anything you do not buy. In fact, the rental business is a pretty good one. You are not the owner; you simply pay for the right to use something.

As a renter, your legal position depends on what sort of arrangement you reach with the lender; that is, the rentor. In real estate this agreement is called a *lease*. You rent certain premises, usually for a fixed period of time—in years, months, or even days.

In the rental of apartments or houses, there are various kinds of arrangements. For example, a *tenancy at will* means that either you or the landlord may terminate the agreement at any time, generally upon thirty days prior notice. Or you may have a fixed time under a lease. Check the law in your state as to the actual termination time.

A lease is probably one of the most misunderstood arrangements today. Tenants feel that it is totally one-sided; that there is no way they could possibly win if any kind of dispute arose. This is not true. A number of

44

books have been published recently on the relationship between tenant and landlord. Some may be applicable to the law in your state and some may not. Where problems have existed because of the signed lease, the public has been testing the legalities in the courts. For example, the apartment owner fails to make certain repairs on the elevator; the tenants are constantly getting stuck. So, the tenants form a committee to talk to the landlord (the apartment owner). Sometimes tenants are successful, but if they are not, legal action could be taken. In certain areas tenant groups have succeeded simply by banding together and then testing the provisions of the lease in court.

The late Leon Amstell, a real-estate attorney in the area of tenant/landlord relations in New York, said that many of the provisions in the "standard" lease today are "against public policy," meaning that if a court ever sunk its teeth into it, the court would find any number of provisions unacceptable.

What is a lease and what does it do?

The basic point to remember is that a lease obligates you as a tenant (and this applies whether it is an apartment or a house) to pay certain sums of money in return for the right to inhabit a specific area. Do you need a lawyer to enter into a lease?

Most of the time, in an apartment rental, a lawyer is not necessary. For example, you search high and low for a particular apartment in a particular area of town at a particular rent. You pound the pavements from dawn to dusk. You call rental agents. You devour the classifieds. Finally, in the third month of your search, you find what you are looking for. And the price is just right.

It now becomes a question of who is hungrier: you or the landlord. If it is a rentor's market (meaning the landlord has a long list of people clamoring for the apartment), and you decide to give him flak, or you hire a lawyer who begins to make too many waves, then it is quite possible that the landlord will not rent to you. He may decide that it is less of a problem to rent to someone who has his money in one hand and a pen to sign the lease in the other.

Be practical, and break it down into logical components. How much rent are you being asked to pay and for what length of time? If you have found yourself a huge, bright, clean studio apartment at $150 a month for a six-month period, you may question why a lawyer would be necessary to go over the lease and possibly "cause problems."

On the other hand, if you are dealing for a $1500-a-month apartment for more than a three-year period, well, why not have a lawyer go over the lease? That's a lot of cash you're paying out and you may need to know what is and what isn't important in that 43-paragraph, 6-page lease thrust in front of you.

But also remember this: Even with a $150-a-month gem, you should still read the lease just to make sure that nothing has been added that might turn the "great deal" into something less favorable. After all, it's still in English, notwithstanding the tiny print.

What then are the most important elements and key points to watch for in a lease?

First, look for certain basics:

1. What is the length of the lease? You say it should be for six months? Okay, then,

2. When does it start and when does it stop? Are those dates included?

3. What do you get for what you are paying? In other words, if it's apartment 3-G at 694 East 11th Street, that should be spelled out.

4. What are you paying? $900? Let it be said.

5. How is it to be paid? $150 at the first of each month? Any extra costs? Any security deposit or a month's rent to be paid in advance? What happens to that advance or security? A number of leases today obligate the landlord under law to put your security in a special account or trust fund and to pay you interest on it.

6. What about privileges? Can you use the laundry room, the garage, the pool, the storage area, the sauna? It should all be stated in the lease. Nothing should be taken for granted.

7. Who is responsible for repairs and upkeep? Are you obligated to do any of this? This is especially important when you are renting a house. For example, who takes care of the Japanese garden? What happens if that big old elm in the backyard dies? Are you responsible for pruning the rose bushes?

And what if there is a fire? Most leases provide that the tenant must notify the landlord, and that he must repair the damage as soon as possible. If the tenant stays on the premises during the repairs, does he continue to pay the rent? If the damages cause the tenant to vacate, does the obligation to pay rent cease?

8. How about a *sublet clause?* This enables you to rent the premises to another person, sometimes with or without the landlord's permission. Is it important? Only you can determine that. What happens if you have to vacate the premises, for whatever reason? Can you?

These are just some of the points that may have to be ironed but before you sign an apartment or house lease.

Also, many leases have what are termed Standard Rules and Regulations attached as a rider, which, if read carefully, seem to be anything but standard. They may prevent you from keeping your baby carriage outside your door, or they may have a restriction against your pet parakeet. And, it doesn't stop just at kids or pets. What about your business?

Suppose you are thinking of turning your new apartment into a photographic studio? Does the lease restrict you from doing that? It would be sad to discover that you can't do any photography work at all on the premises AFTER you have spent a fortune for equipment.

With these things in mind can you determine if you really need a lawyer. But again, it depends. If you are adept at reading leases—or you are in an area where leases are being prepared in nontechnical terms (a number of insurance companies are now doing this with their policies)—and also understand what the lease says and what you can or cannot live with, you may not need a lawyer. But, when in doubt, consult one.

Okay, you have signed the lease on that dream apartment, and it has become a nightmare. The woman upstairs plays rock music on her eight-track stereo in the middle of the night, the toilet whines incessantly, the heating system can't be regulated and you're sitting in a 110-degree room in the middle of July, and in order to turn on the bathroom light, you have to ring the doorbell. You decide it's time to get out.

You have to be careful about breaking leases, and we're not advocating that you do so. Bear in mind that your state may have laws that favor the landlord, your complaints notwithstanding. Therefore, even though you *think* you may have a reason for walking away from the premises, you should double-check your legal position. You could wind up in even greater trouble by illegally breaking a lease.

Of course, the reverse has to be considered too. Suppose the landlord is trying to get rid of you? Obviously, he has the right to evict anyone who is violating a substantial portion of the lease (the most frequent cause being failure to pay the rent), but the laws differ in various jurisdictions. For example, one state has a law mandating that a landlord must go to court and *ask* the court to evict the tenant. Another state says no court approval is necessary.

The question, of course, as to whether you may always be evicted for violation of the landlord's rules and regulations is a difficult one to answer because of these different laws.

To cite another illustration, in one state a landlord could evict you if the rules specifically said "No Pets" and you kept a gerbil, while in a neighboring state the court says you could keep the pet notwithstanding a restriction in the lease.

However, you must be practical, realistic, and somewhat conscious of your time and money before you proceed with any legal action to enforce your rights. Remember, a lawyer's time is worth money, and so is yours. Make sure the matter is worth it.

Let's look at some of the problems.

Most of the arguments between landlords and tenants revolve around either (1) the past-due rent or (2) the return of the security deposit.

It is an understatement to say that landlords generally do not like to wait for their rent money. Sometimes, though, they are forced to. This is where tenants can form a group to protest certain tactics of the landlord. One effective way is the collective nonpayment of rent. Everybody decides not to pay.

CAUTION: Rent strikes and other strategies are really beyond the scope of this book and require expert advice, from an attorney well versed in landlord-tenant relations.

But, the most frequent kinds of landlord-tenant disputes (at least from your side) concern the return of security deposits.

When you leave the premises at the end of your lease, you are supposed to get back your security deposit; in fact, under many laws being passed throughout the country, those deposits are to be held in special accounts with the interest to be paid to you.

Landlords like to protect themselves fully. The original reason for a security deposit was to protect the landlord against damage to the premises: stained wallpaper, holes in the ceiling, broken bathroom tiles. A problem arises when the landlord and the tenant disagree as to "damage." Can the landlord keep the entire security deposit or withhold a portion of it?

When it comes to damage, understand that you are generally *not* liable for "normal wear and tear." That is a rather nebulous phrase, but a little wear and tear on the rugs, or dirty venetian blinds, or a worn washer on the faucet doesn't exactly constitute a mutilation of the premises, warranting the withholding of the security.

But what can you do when the landlord does not pay you back? One of the simplest methods is to sue the landlord in small claims court. (See Chapter 9 for the procedure involved.) However, watch this carefully. Some leases provide for a waiver of certain kinds of legal action, such as waiver of trial by jury. In any event, small claims court is a relatively easy and convenient way to settle such a dispute.

Remember, too, that the landlord will be bound by the same legal rules of damages as you are. This means that he must prove his damages, and therefore he can collect only the value of the damaged items, or their reasonable repair cost. Of course, if you feel the landlord is asking for monies way above what you feel the damage warrants, then by all means get your own estimate and take it to court.

What happens if you decide to leave *before* your lease expires? Can you get your security back?

In most states, if you break the lease, the landlord is under no obligation to rerent the apartment. Theoretically, then, he can wait until the end of the lease and hold you responsible for all the rent due. By the same token, provisions in many states now obligate the landlord to try to *mitigate* the damages. In other words, he must attempt to rerent the premises, and if he does, you are not responsible for that rent, provided that the new tenant is paying at least the same amount.

Naturally you can try to rent it yourself. If you have a sublet clause in your lease, this is much easier to do, but even if you don't, you should look for ways to minimize your liability. Remember, you are trying to relieve yourself of that lease and to get back the security, if you can. But you can do this only by showing that the landlord is not "out-of-pocket"; that he hasn't lost any money by your leaving. Once you are able to accomplish this, then you can go after the security deposit. Again, you may find yourself in small claims court.

There is another side of the argument too. The landlord may raise the specter of penalty: "You relinquish your security in return for my relinquishing the lease."

Your argument? You might take the position that a penalty clause is against the law. This shifts the burden onto the landlord to prove that it isn't. The key is that if you can show that the landlord is *not* being hurt, that he is *not* out any money, you should be able to get your security deposit back.

Another aspect: How do you get money from a landlord who has *cost* you money? For example, if the landlord has a duty to repair certain items pursuant to your lease, then he is liable for the "reasonably foreseeable consequences of that duty." Suppose you notify him to repair the refrigerator, but he fails to do so. As a result, your food spoils and the water leaks through to the apartment below, damaging that tenant's property. Looks like good grounds for a lawsuit?

Again, your best recourse may be small claims court. There is one caveat here: If personal injuries are involved—if you slip on the water and injure yourself—you may take action for not only personal injury but also for pain and suffering. At this point you are no longer in small claims court, and you should consult an attorney to determine your rights and the type of lawsuit you can file.

No discussion about landlord/tenant relations would be complete without mentioning something about the landlord's side. Landlords have rights, and these also can be exercised in small claims court. For example, if the tenant owes rent (or money for damages to your premises), the landlord too can take the matter into court.

Defaults of one kind or another by a tenant are usually the most common problems for the landlord. The use of a lawyer? A number of landlords tell us that initially they use a lawyer to help set up the standard set of forms, such as leases, and at times to help "coach" in situations involving defaults. The lawyer devises a system for the landlord to follow in default situations:

> You are owed three hundred dollars.
> Send form letter A.
> Wait ten days.
> Send form letter B.
> Wait three days.
> Go to court and fill out form XYZ.

The landlord gets it down pat the first time and he is off and running. He may not need the lawyer again.

Surveys show that the general amount a landlord sues for is under $400, an amount appropriate for small claims court. (There is no minimum in this court, only a maximum. See the Appendix for Chapter 9.) A landlord can do pretty well here once he knows the ropes, and those "ropes" can be secured from his attorney.

BUYING & SELLING

Nearly everyone at some time in his life faces the problems of buying and selling real estate, whether it is a house, cooperative, or condominium. In fact, according to the American Bar Association survey, for every 1,000 adults, 710 acquire real property. For the most part, this involves the purchase of a home, which is probably the largest single investment a person will ever undertake. In certain Sunbelt communities around the country condominiums are purchased, and in larger urban areas it's cooperative apartments.

In any real-estate transaction, the seller, the real-estate broker, and the bank may have an attorney representing each of their interests. An attorney representing any of these parties (even though you may be charged a fee for that person, as in the case of a bank) is still not *your* attorney. You have to protect your own interests whether you're selling or buying, and particularly if you're buying

There is much to be considered when buying property. What are the tax rates? What are the zoning ordinances? What are the public services? How about transportation, highways, shopping, medical services? The list can seem endless.

It may very well be that you can't get all the answers you need from one source, such as an attorney. Possibly you'll need to talk to real-estate agents, local officials, and community planners in order to get an idea of what kind of area you are moving into.

The initial question is whether or not you need a lawyer to buy a house? Here there is no clear and definitive answer. For example, in California there are escrow and title companies that handle all aspects of house buying and rarely are lawyers involved. In fact, according to lawyers interviewed in California, virtually no one uses them. Is this a mistake? One attorney said it is. "The purchase of a home is important and runs more smoothly when lawyers are involved."

In the East, especially in the Northeast, lawyers are an integral part of house-buying, and their services are valued. There is no question that under *ideal* conditions, you can select a house, bargain for it, sign the contract for sale, take possession of it, and live there happily ever after with no problem and without the aid of a lawyer.

One couple on Long Island did it. In 1966, they bought a Levitt-made house, putting 5 percent down and carrying a 30-year conventional mortgage. In fact, they didn't even have to secure the mortgage from the bank. The builder had the arrangement well in hand for everyone who qualified. The couple simply appeared on the day of closing, many papers were passed their way, plus a duplicate set of house keys (front, back, and garage), and they had a house. It was as easy as that, and the only lawyer they saw that day was the one representing the bank. Actually, he represented everyone. A few years later, the couple sold their house to a real-estate agent, and no lawyers were present except the agent's. More papers were passed around and everyone went home happy.

Of course, then there is the story of another couple who bought a nice big house and decided to do everything themselves. They wound up in the biggest pickle possible. They signed contracts which obligated them all over the lot, and when they tried to pull out of the deal because they discovered termites, they were told, "No, no." Apparently, they had waived their rights when they signed an agreement to buy "as is." This meant they had contracted to buy the house in whatever condition they found it. The onus—the responsibility of inspections, surveys, and the like—rested solely on the couple.

The bottom line is that unless you know what you are doing or know how to do it (including what to look for), a lawyer is important.

But you can find out what to do. Another couple went to a lawyer to buy a house on the outskirts of Chicago. When they decided to sell the house many years later, they went to the same lawyer. They paid close attention to what was being done in both procedures. They asked a lot of questions and were careful to understand every step involved.

Years later, they decided to buy again. This time they called the lawyer to ask if any aspects of the law had been changed. Then, they went ahead and did it themselves—and with great success. But remember, they spent time and energy in researching aspects of real-estate buying and knew what to do and what to expect, and they touched base with their lawyer whenever they were in doubt.

Of course, this couple represents the exception, not the rule. Thus, unless you know what you are doing and care to know, plus have a penchant for organization, stay out of it. Consult a lawyer.

In real estate you are dealing with binders, contracts, deposits, escrows, deeds, mortgages, titles, so let's follow this along.

You are looking for a fully air-conditioned Tudor-style house with four bedrooms, two bathrooms, a modern kitchen, two fireplaces, a finished recreation room, and all on two wooded acres near transportation and shopping. Of course, it should also be in a top-rated school area with low taxes and full services. And, you find it.

At this stage, you'll probably be asked to sign a *binder* or *purchase agreement* and pay a deposit, generally known as *earnest money*.

In effect, the binder is a memorandum between you and the seller, and it contains the basic terms of the arrangement. The binder may be prepared by either the buyer or the seller, and it may include certain provisions that are unacceptable to you.

But wait a minute. A binder or purchase agreement is more than a mere receipt for a deposit. It is actually a contract, and is a legally enforceable and *binding* agreement. However, in some jurisdictions, such as Connecticut, a binder *is* treated as a receipt (sometimes called "earnest money"), and is fully refundable. Thus, it is important to check the law in your state as to how binders and purchase agreements are considered. Some states consider a binder a valid contract; some say it is only a receipt for money.

Of course you shouldn't sign any document or pay any money until you understand all your obligations in the transaction. The purchase agreement you do sign should spell out all of the terms of the sale; for example, the purchase price, how it is to be paid, the amount of cash required, the way it is to be financed, the interest charges, and so forth.

A check list of what the agreement should contain includes:

1. The purchase price
2. When it is to be paid
3. Description of the property, plus a breakdown of all items (carpet, drapes, etc.) to be included
4. Who pays what part of the taxes and insurance, or any other costs
5. Date on which you take possession
6. Commitment for the seller to furnish title warranty
7. Type of deed to be furnished, plus a marketable title to the property
8. What happens if you can't get a mortgage
9. What happens if the deal collapses for whatever other reason

Attorneys representing a buyer suggest that the purchase agreement should provide for you to cancel if you can't get financing. (If you're the seller, however, you may not want the buyer to have that cancellation privilege.) The question obviously revolves around what happens to your intital payment (the down payment) if the deal falls through. The payment of a deposit in which the purchase price is stated by you to a third party (say, to the broker as the agent for the seller) to hold in escrow should suffice until you and the seller can negotiate the agreement.

A *contract of sale* usually follows this stage, and this document spells out in detail the rights and obligations of the parties. Keep in mind that the laws regarding real property dictate that all matters be put in writing. Accordingly, any items agreed upon by the parties but *not* included in the written contract will *not* be admitted into evidence if a lawsuit should arise. Agreements for the sale of houses and of all real property MUST be in writing.

Before you prepare for a closing, you should understand the elements involved: title, taxes, special assessments, title searches, title insurance, surveys.

What is *title* to a property? This is what you get at the closing. Title is the right of the owner to its peaceful possession and use, free from the claims of others. Therefore, when you buy a home, you should be certain that you have the right to occupy it without legal interference from anyone. And you should also have the right to sell or mortgage it without problems. In other words, you want a clear and unencumbered ownership to your property.

There are a number of ways in which the use of your property may be limited, however. One is by a restriction in the deed; another is by local zoning laws. Almost all land is subject to real property taxes, which, if they are not paid, could result in the loss of title. Other debts owed on the property, such as special assessments or levies, can also cause problems later on.

Title searches then are exactly what they say they are. You should satisfy yourself that the seller can convey a *marketable title* to the property to you as agreed upon in the purchase contract. Various methods ensure that the title received from the seller is marketable. One protection is through *title insurance.*

Title insurance simply insures that the title is free and clear, so if there's a judgment later on, you will not be held accountable.

The Federal Housing Administration estimates that there are some 1,000 possible claims that could be made against property ownership. These range from forged deeds to liens of builders to "missing" owners. Title insurance provides a protection in the way of defending your title in court or settling any valid claims. In effect, it gives you financial protection against loss of your property and the possible expense of defending its title in court.

The *deed* is the document that actually conveys or transfers title from one person to another. For the most part, there are three types of deeds:

* The *bargain and sale deed* is one in which the seller makes no express covenants as to the title he is conveying. He warrants that he has a marketable title and that he is transferring that to you, the buyer.

* The *full convenant and warranty deed* is one in which the seller promises and warrants that you will enjoy the ownership and use of the property, and that no one will interfere with or dispute that right. If there is an outside claim of title, the seller will then be financially responsible for any damage or loss sustained by you. This is otherwise known as the covenant of "quiet enjoyment."

* The *quitclaim deed* is used primarily to release any claims that one may have against the property. This deed usually gives the buyer those rights and interests as only the seller has in the property. Such a deed, when recorded, will generally remove any claim against the property that may exist on the record.

The *closing* on the purchase of a home is the transaction in which you receive all the documents (as outlined above) required to convey the title to you. These documents should be reviewed carefully to make sure that the conditions and promises of the purchase contract are being fulfilled.

Also, at this time, the balance of the purchase price is paid to the seller. Additionally, arrangements are made at the closing as to when you will occupy your new home. Normally, when the full purchase price is paid, the keys to the house are delivered to the buyer on the spot, and he has the right to move in immediately.

However, your purchase contract may specify that you move in at a later date. Make sure it conforms to your needs.

The important thing to remember is that buying a house is a major investment. It usually involves making payments over a period of many years. In the long run, it may be more economical to have competent legal advice in making the purchase than to risk the trouble and expense that could result from not having that advice in the first place. In any event, it is your own responsibility to seek the guidance of someone knowledgeable in this field in order to protect yourself and to see that what you get is what you are legally entitled to receive.

What can you expect to pay in the way of legal fees for buying or selling real estate? This varies considerably but based on the authors' survey, you might run across the following sums: For an examination of a title, the fee is generally calculated on the amount risked: for the owner, that is considered the purchase price; for the buyer, it is the amount loaned.

For instance, $ 25,000–50,000: $3/8$ of 1% (as the fee)

50,000–100,000: $1/4$ of 1%

100,000–500,000: $2/10$ of 1%

For closings, a great number of lawyers charge about $10 for each $1,000 of the sale price, but again, this varies depending on where you are.

Two alternatives now exist with respect to purchasing a home in the suburbs or in leasing an apartment in the city. These alternatives apply to condominiums and cooperatives, and the forms of ownership in these two areas have certain tax advantages over merely leasing space.

CONDOMINIUMS

Condominiums are usually apartment houses where *plans of purchase* are offered. In a condominium an individual owns the space in which he lives, but he shares all of the responsibilities—and benefits—with the other occupants of the apartment building and condominium site. The ownership is in the form of a corporation that is financed by you and the other owners who pay monthly assessments for maintenance and for the use of areas in the site: driveways, garages, recreation halls, swimming pools, hallways, and the like.

Rules for the participants are enforced by a Board of Directors. If there is a violation, the condominium owner may be fined by the Board of Directors. To put it another way, with a condominium arrangement you buy your apartment, and at the same time you buy into all the community facilities, including such items as swimming pools and recreation halls.

However, as good as it all sounds, there are problems. Many scams have taken place with regard to recreational condominiums. One of the forms these usually take is as follows:

You buy a condominium in lovely downtown Ft. Lauderdale. It is a glorious pink-colored apartment complex with a swimming pool and golf club. But, as part of the deal and as part of the condominium ownership, the seller includes a clause that all of the maintenance for the pool and golf club (plus all equipment) would be leased through, or maintained by, a corporation owned by the sponsor or seller. This means that you will pay extra for the operation of such facilities and that the services are *not* going to be controlled by you. Sometimes rates to be paid are extremely high, and you are locked into maintenance charges for recreational facilities that are exorbitant compared with the area's prevailing rates. Actually the *sponsors* are the managers of the property. And the managerial fees can be steep.

Therefore, you must be concerned with not only the cost in acquiring your apartment but also the costs involved in the accessory or ancillary benefits of the condominium.

If you invest a substantial amount of your savings for a condominium or use a portion of your pension plan monies for a retirement home, you should consult an attorney, and it should be an attorney who represents you, not the sponsor.

Just as in the purchase of a home, a condominium is usually financed with a down payment upon the signing of a contract, with the balance to be paid at the closing of title. This balance can be a bank mortgage. There are many tax advantages to the purchase of a condominium (deduction of expenses for repairs, maintenance, depreciation, bank interest charges), but there are many inherent dangers too. Although a number of governmental agencies in most states regulate the sale of condominiums, great care should be placed in checking out the track record of the sponsor as well as in examining what the sponsor is offering and what charges would be incurred.

In short, BE CAREFUL, and consult a lawyer.

COOPERATIVES

With a cooperative a corporation is formed (usually a nonprofit one) to purchase from the sponsor-seller certain land and an apartment building. Ownership of the apartment corporation's shares entitle the buyer to a special lease on an apartment, commonly known as a proprietary lease.

As a shareholder, you have the right to vote annually for the Board of Directors, which then conducts the affairs of the apartment corporation and supervises the operation of the property.

As the lessee, you pay an amount customarily called *maintenance charges*, which represents your proportionate share of the apartment corporation's cash requirements for the operation and maintenance of the property, as well as for the creation of a reserve for contingencies (building or repairs) that the Board of Directors may deem proper.

It works like this: Blocks of shares allocated to various apartments in your building are offered for sale at so many dollars per share. Each buyer is required to pay a certain amount of money, called "additional cash payment," to enable the apartment corporation to acquire the property. In other words, the tenants form a group to buy the property from the owner. Usually, the number of shares allocated to each apartment and the amount of such additional payment due from the buyer are set forth in a schedule in the prospectus offered by the sponsor-seller. The estimated annual maintenance charges for each apartment are also set forth in the prospectus.

Many apartment houses become cooperatives after a period of a few years when the sponsor-seller wants to make a profit from his building of the building. The share of the purchase price of an additional cash payment is usually lower for tenants already in residence than for outsiders. Of course, you should determine if the purchase price to you as a tenant already in possession *is* lower. This can vary, but the general sum is a 20-percent discount. The price may vary according to the size of the apartment and whether it's on a lower or higher floor. A large apartment on a higher floor costs more because it's considered to be more desirable.

As soon as you have decided to buy, you will have to apply to the bank for a mortgage, just as you would if you were buying a house. All decisions with respect to the acceptance or rejection of the loan applications will be made solely by the bank. The documents and procedures to effectuate the loan will conform to the bank's requirements for cooperative loans. Interest rates change from time to time, as do the terms for repayment. If you're lucky, you might obtain a thirty-year mortgage, but this will depend on your area.

A person who wants to purchase shares in an apartment-corporation usually must sign what is commonly called a *subscription agreement*. This is written evidence of the tenant's intention to purchase. The subscription agreement is accompanied by an amount of money equal to the number of shares the tenant will be acquiring in the apartment-corporation. The sponsor-seller will then hold all the monies received by him directly, or through his agent, in a special escrow account until the necessary legal evidences of purchase have been obtained.

In many jurisdictions there must be a minimum number of tenants interested in purchasing shares in the cooperative apartment and obtaining proprietary leases on their apartments before the plan will be effective. Once the plan is effective, though, the seller will apprise the tenant, and they will proceed to *contract*, where the tenant formally commits himself to the purchase of his apartment share. Then, appropriate financing is obtained, and a closing is held in order to transfer the shares and the property lease to the tenant.

Under present tax laws you are entitled to deduct from your adjusted gross income on your federal, city, or state income tax returns, your proportionate share of the real-estate taxes paid by the apartment-corporation, including interest paid during the taxable year. This seems simple enough, but it is recommended that you consult an accountant prior to the acquisition of a cooperative so that he can assess, based upon the prospectus of the sponsor-seller and based upon your gross adjusted income, to what advantage or disadvantage you may have in acquiring a cooperative. A cooperative isn't for everybody.

Moreover, a situation may arise where you like the building in which you are living but would like to purchase a larger apartment on a higher floor. Care should be given in reading the prospectus that there are provisions permitting you as a tenant-occupant to substitute an apartment at a discounted price.

There are conflicting opinions as to whether one requires an attorney to effectuate the acquisition of a cooperative. Many feel that if the situation is set forth in a fair manner by a good, qualified sponsor, there is no need for an attorney. Others feel that since your fellow tenants are purchasing what you are, there is nothing wrong with the deal. This is known as safety in numbers or "apathy by majority."

There is no doubt that if you are expending substantial sums of money, the services of an attorney should be obtained from the inception in order to protect your interests.

TO SUMMARIZE

Real property is concerned with land and those items that are a permanent part of the land, such as buildings. Property may be owned by one person or by a number of persons. If it is acquired by a group, then the nature of the ownership will determine their respective rights. Transactions concerning real property are more strict and more formal. than many other arrangements.

Here are some additional questions that need to be answered in buying or leasing real property:

1. If you are buying a house, does the binder that the seller wants you to sign deprive you of any rights before you even sign the purchase contract?

2. Is there an existing mortgage? Do you have to assume it? Can you get your own mortgage?

3. Are there any restrictions that may deprive you of the proper enjoyment or use of the property?

4. What kind of deed are you getting?

5. If you are leasing property, what restrictions are imposed in the lease? Do they prevent you from carrying on your business? In fact, is there any zoning or other restriction that has been established by the community that may prevent you from actually operating a business?

6. Are there any rules and regulations in small print on the back of your lease that may limit you in the use and enjoyment of your premises?

7. Do you want a jury trial in the event there is a dispute with your landlord?

8. Is there an automatic-renewal clause in your lease? Is there an option to renew? What about any items that you attach to the premises? Do they become part of that property when the lease is terminated?

And this can go on and on. Do you need a lawyer?

As you can gather by now, except for certain minor situations as outlined in this chapter, transactions involving real property can become very complicated: They require a good number of legal documents and involve specific technical procedures. More real-property arrangements, then, cry out for a competent, qualified attorney.

5

Business Relationships

Suppose your best friend proposes that the two of you go into the mail-order business. Or suppose you decide to open your own shop. Or suppose you and a group of wealthy individuals want to purchase a professional baseball team. What do you have to know before you go into business for yourself or with anyone else? What do you have to watch out for? What are your liabilities? What are your responsibilities? And, perhaps most importantly, do you need a lawyer?

The three basic forms of business arrangements are individual ownership, the partnership, and the corporation. Of course, the simplest way is to open up a store and begin rendering a service by just using your name; for example, John Jones, florist. However, in order to determine whether you need a lawyer and what is involved in opening a business, you should understand these three forms of business arrangements.

INDIVIDUAL OWNERSHIP

Individual ownership, or sole proprietorship, simply means that you (and anyone else with you) form a business. You put up the money and you are the boss. For example, "John Jones, doing business as John's Florist Shop." The "doing business as," sometimes referred to as the d/b/a, means you are doing business under another name.

Do you need an attorney to do this? For the most part, no. All you have to do is fill out a business certificate, which can be obtained commercially, and file it with the clerk in the county court. In some instances you may have to obtain a license to operate a certain kind of business, but that can be secured from the appropriate government agency. Unless the business is complex, a lawyer is usually unnecessary.

Of course, if you are buying an existing business, you may need the advice of an attorney or, at the very least, of an accountant. In this case, you should know whether there are any unpaid taxes or liens against the business for which you might be held liable. By the same token, what about the premises? Are you renting, buying, or what? And under what circumstances? The law in your area may require you to publish a notice of the transfer of the business in the local newspapers, and, accordingly, you may face a penalty if you don't comply.

Many variables exist here, but a number of elements must be considered before you go into business for yourself. For example, suppose you want to be a professional photographer. Do you know what licenses are required, what insurance you have to carry, the forms of agreements you should use, what your liabilities and obligations are? It's not simply a matter of picking up a camera and taking pictures. Perhaps an attorney is not necessary. You may be able to contact another professional photographer who is knowledgeable about the business aspects and set up your studio based on his advice. An accountant might also be consulted. The point is that you may need some sort of guidance, and you shouldn't hesitate to obtain it.

More than half of the businesses in the United States are sole proprietorships. These range from newsstands to drug stores, from barbershops to saloons. The owner is his (or her) own boss, and he reaps the rewards from the fruits of his labors. Of course, he also incurs all losses and is liable for debts. This means that if you own a house and don't have enough money in the bank to pay those business bills, it's possible that you can be sued and liens put on your house. In fact, the house can be taken to pay off part of the debts." As Peter R. Cella, a prominent New York attorney, advised, "Careful consideration should be given in selecting by what means you should conduct your business."

PARTNERSHIPS

A partnership is a step more complicated than individual ownership. One of the primary differences between the two forms is that a partnership is subject to a specific written agreement among the participants.

Each of the partners invests his money and his time as co-owner of a business.

In partnership the parties agree that they will share the proceeds of any profits, and, conversely, they share the debts. Thus, each person is liable for the debts of the partnership. Partnerships are formed for a number of reasons. For instance, one party may have the money, and the other may have the goods.

In a partnership each general partner is the manager of the business and usually has one vote no matter how much money he has contributed. In effect, there is really no boss. Each partner is the agent of the other partner carrying on the business and as such can bind the partnership by his own act. Of course, there are some safeguards here. There are certain things that partners cannot do on their own. A partner cannot give away any partnership property to creditors without approval of the other partners, and he certainly cannot relinquish the goodwill (the name and spirit of the business) of the partnership. In short, he cannot do anything that would make it impossible to carry on the business.

Two basic types of partnerships are the *general partnership*, where the partners share equally in the management of the business, including the losses, profits, responsibilities, and obligations and the *limited partnership*, where a certain partner's liability is limited. Usually, that partner puts up some money initially and then steps back from the daily operation of the business. For example, you could invest money with no control over how the business is to be run. You simply have a profit participation. If the business succeeds, you make money; if it turns to worms, then you lose your investment.

Normally, a limited partner is not liable for more than his original investment. However, under some arrangements he may have some liability for additional money. For example, you can provide in the limited-partnership agreement that in the event more money is needed for the business, the limited partner can be called on for such sums. This is sometimes called an "override," and it obligates the limited partner to invest an additional sum in order for the business to continue or to pay off specific debts. This is not mandatory in all such agreements, and it is totally negotiable.

Suppose you decide to get out of a partnership. Will you still be liable for all the debts? No. You will have to give all of the people you do business with written notice that you are no longer a partner, and then you will be liable only for the debts contracted before you leave the business. In fact, creditors must try to get all of their monies from the partnership before they attempt to go after you personally.

What if you want to bring somebody new into the business? Will that party be liable for prior debts? Any new investor is liable for debts contracted by the partnership only *after* he becomes a partner. However, any monies he puts in could be used to satisfy existing debts.

The next question is a logical one. How do partnerships end? In a number of ways: One of the partners (in a two-man operation) may be declared to be mentally incapacitated by the court, or one of the partners may go bankrupt, or under other conditions specified in the agreement.

Two additional aspects should be considered. First, there is really no specific way that a partner can protect himself from major liability in a partnership arrangement except under the terms of the specific partnership agreement or by the use of insurance coverage. Second, it should be recognized that one partner can go bankrupt without the other. This means that an individual can have a personal bankruptcy that would not affect the partnership as a whole. However, if the partnership goes bankrupt, then that condition applies to all the partners.

This now raises the question as to whether or not you need a lawyer to enter into a partnership agreement. Yes and no. You definitely need a lawyer if you are talking about a complex situation involving both general and limited partners with different types of liability for each party. You may not need a lawyer, though, for a simple partnership of two general partners sharing equally down the line.

Most partnerships are formed by a written agreement called *articles of partnership*. This includes (1) the names of the partners, (2) firm name, (3) place of business, (4) kind of business, (5) term of the arrangement, (6) amount invested by each partner, (7) sharing arrangement on profits and losses, (8) accounting system, and (9) termination method. The minimum cost of a lawyer to draw up a partnership agreement is usually about $150.

CORPORATIONS

While the largest and most important American businesses are corporations, so are some of the smallest. A corporation is merely a group of people who have banded together to do business. They obtain a charter from the state, which grants them, as a unit, some powers and liabilities for conducting a specific activity. In effect, the law regards a corporation as an individual, and, as such, a corporation may own, buy, sell, and inherit property in its own name. Its liability is also limited: The members are exempt from personal liability beyond the amount of their individual shares.

How is a corporation constructed? Investors become, by virtue of their investment, the shareholders of the company. As shareholders, they elect the Board of Directors, whose responsibility is to see to the day-to-day management of the corporation.

Consider a corporation to be a pie owned by two people. If the pie is sliced in eight pieces, each shareholder can get four for putting in an equal amount of money. Or they may decide to take only three slices each, leaving two extra slices in the event they want to bring in more money later on by selling them to someone else. The key, however, is to retain a controlling interest; thus, as long as the two shareholders control at least six pieces, they control the corporation. To set up this group, they have to file a *certificate of incorporation* with the Secretary of State in their state. Most jurisdictions require three or more parties to incorporate, although in a few states one person is enough.

The certificate includes: (1) the name of the corporation, (2) the type of business, (3) where the office will be, (4) the total amount of the shares to be authorized, (5) the value of each share, and a few other items of that sort. It is not a difficult form to complete.

In addition to the certificate of incorporation, it is also necessary to write up by-laws. These are regulations detailing the duties of the members of the corporation. They set forth the time and place of all meetings, the voting rights of the members, the way amendments to the corporate papers can be made, and other rules covering the business, including the dividend schedules of various classes of stock.

In a simple corporation an arrangement is usually made for a 200-no-par-value share. This means that the stock has no value ascribed to it, and therefore no share receives preference over another. Actually that's normally the way small business corporations are devised. It keeps things uncomplicated. Small business corporations have both advantages and disadvantages. If the corporation loses money, the parties can't write off the loss on their personal income tax returns. Some tax laws, however, do allow small corporations with ten or fewer stockholders to offset corporate losses against their personal losses for tax purposes. But these laws also make the small corporation responsible to pay for profits as though they were personal property. The arrangement is known as a *Subchapter S Corporation*, and the real benefit is that it can deduct certain expenses that a sole proprietor cannot. For example, it can set up a profit-sharing plan, a pension plan, and a health insurance plan, all of which are considered legitimate business expenses.

How do you decide where to incorporate, and is it necessary to incorporate everywhere?

As a rule, you should seek incorporation in the state in which you do most of your business. You can be located in one state and do business elsewhere, and it isn't necessary to incorporate everywhere you do business. Do you really need a lawyer then? You can probably do a lot of the work yourself.

Some companies print certificate-of-incorporation forms, including by-laws, and it's simply a matter of obtaining them and filling in the blanks. However, the legal requirements for forming businesses vary from state to state.

A number of lawyers today offer cut-rate services to anyone who wants to form a corporation, and a simple arrangement may cost under $100.

TERMINATING A BUSINESS

Do you need a lawyer in order to terminate your business? Sometimes not. It may be a simple procedure. First you must satisfy any contracts you may have. Then you gather in all your assets, sell your equipment and stock, and pay off your debts. Finally, you lock the door. That's it. The business is finished. You don't need anyone's permission to do that, and you certainly don't need a lawyer. Of course, if you have a business with 100 employees, 42 directors, and 120,000 shares of stock, it may be more complex.

A similar procedure also applies if you die, in which case, the money realized by the liquidation (or sale) of your business would become part of your estate, and it would then be distributed by your executor as provided in your will.

However, a business doesn't always have to be liquidated just because the owner dies. You may have provided in your will for it to pass on to a relative or friend. If that sounds good to you, then you may want to explore the various avenues of passing on ownership in order to make the best disposition of property after your death. (see Chapter 8.)

Dissolving a partnership or a corporation requires closer examination. For example, certain aspects of the law must be considered. A partnership does not cease to exist on a legal basis simply because you decide to dissolve it. Actually, it remains in existence until its affairs have been settled, then it automatically terminates.

During the winding-up (or winding-down) period, the partners usually have no legal right and authority to enter into a new business. Their role in the business is primarily that of trustees, and their job is to see that unfinished business is completed: accounts audited, accounts receivable collected, inventory, fixtures, and other property liquidated, and the proceeds properly distributed.

Naturally this assumes that the partnership was solvent upon dissolution. If your partnership has failed, then the partners must draw on their personal resources to pay the debts owed to the firm's creditors. Thus, unless there is some other understanding, all must contribute equally to the satisfaction of these debts.

Back to the partnership arrangement: It is important, therefore, that the agreement between the partners spells out in detail all the conditions, rights, and obligations of the parties. It will save a lot of heartache later on. Do you need a lawyer to do that? Not if you can do it yourself.

Dissolving a corporation is trickier. Like a partnership, a corporation does not go out of business as soon as its owners decide to terminate it. The law provides a certain period for settling the entity. Sometimes the corporation can be dissolved rather easily by filing a dissolution paper with the Secretary of State (the same party with whom you originally filed the certificate of incorporation), and this you may be able to do yourself. Other times, it may involve something more complicated, in which case the services of a lawyer would be appropriate.

The pivotal point is that you must know what is involved under the laws of your state before dissolving a corporate structure. The Secretary of State can tell you that.

BANKRUPTCY

Within this area are two routes that can be taken: voluntary bankruptcy and involuntary bankruptcy.

If a business cannot pay its debts, it can voluntarily petition the U.S. District Court to declare it a bankrupt. A *bankrupt* means anyone unable to pay his debts. What happens is that a trustee is then appointed by your creditors or by the court, and this trustee collects the assets, sells them, and distributes the proceeds among the creditors.

The creditors, if they agree, are generally paid a certain amount on each dollar owed. For example, suppose a certain business owes you $500. You have a choice of getting nothing when the business closes, or perhaps the trustee will offer you 50¢ on each dollar from the assets collected. In other words, half of what is owed is better than nothing at all.

Naturally you do not have to go automatically into bankruptcy simply because your business is in financial difficulty. You can file a petition to reorganize the business, or you can make an arrangement with your creditors that will enable you to continue in operation and gradually repay them. The bottom line is this: In an involuntary bankruptcy, your creditors file the petition. In a voluntary bankruptcy, you do. An interesting sidelight here is that if you are employed elsewhere and declare yourself a bankrupt, you can't be fired from your job.

A bankruptcy is commenced by filing a petition in federal court in either the area where the business is located or where you live. This petition is a list of all the monies you owe and all the assets you have. You also have to give the court your personal background and the location of your bank accounts. If you are married and own property in both your and your spouse's names, you both may be liable for the debts. The petition has to be signed and notarized. If you lie, you could be charged with perjury.

After the petition is filed the court usually advises your creditors by mail that you are filing for bankruptcy. They then have the right to meet to question you about your financial affairs. A trustee is appointed, and it's up to him to gather your assets together and reduce them to cash in order to pay off the creditors.

Bankruptcy should be used only when you have no other choice, because your credit will suffer afterward.

A number of books on the market cover do-it-yourself bankruptcy. But, look at it this way: If you owe $10,000 and have only $5,000, and you can list all of your assets totaling that $5,000 on the petition statement, you probably can do it yourself rather easily. Clerks of the bankruptcy court are extremely helpful in assisting individuals and small businesses who are filing for bankruptcy.

The key, then, is how complicated it is. That corporation with 42 directors, 100 employees, and 120,000 shares of stock is not going to be easy, while the photographer with one room, two cameras, and six rolls of film will certainly not be difficult.

Only you can determine what help you will need. Check with the court personnel. But when in doubt, don't take chances. Seek the advice and guidance of competent counsel. Lawyers will charge from $150 and up for a personal bankruptcy. It will depend on the complexity of the petition.

COPYRIGHTS, PATENTS, AND TRADEMARKS

Suppose you do succeed? Suppose your business takes off and you are able to do well selling calendars with photographs of animals. How do you prevent somebody else from copying your specific idea? The answer is to copyright what you have created.

There are three areas of property protection that confuse most people: copyright, patent, and trademark. One way to explain the difference is to look at a camera. The way the camera is made is protected by a patent; this means that another company can't come along and copy what has been done. The basic workings of that particular camera, its mechanism, is patented. Inventions then are usually patented.

To patent something, you must go through certain formalities and file certain documents with the Patent Office in Washington, D.C. Yes. Patent law is a highly complicated and specialized branch of law. It would be close to insanity to try to do it without a lawyer.

Now the manufacturer of that camera is protected by a trademark. A trademark is an arbitrary symbol, word, or phrase devised and used by a manufacturer or dealer to designate his goods and understood by the consuming public as denoting those particular goods and distinguishing them from other commodities of a similar kind. For example, Paramount Pictures produces and distributes motion-picture films. Its trademark is the mountain, clouds, stars, and the word "Paramount" scripted across them. That logo, or symbol, represents its product and means that Paramount has an exclusive right to use that logo on its goods in a particular channel of trade.

Trademark registration is under the jurisdiction of the Commissioner of Patents, and, like patents, it requires the services of an expert in the field to effect trademark protection. The Commissioner of Patents issues an instruction booklet for those interested in securing trademark registration of a particular logo, symbol, word, or phrase. But the recommendation is that you retain the services of counsel when dipping into these highly technical waters.

Copyright, however, is a different story.

Going back to the camera, the product of that camera—the photograph—is the item that would be copyrighted. It is a rather uncomplicated operation to copyright the calendars you will be producing. Once you start manufacturing them and offering them for sale, you should fill out the appropriate forms and send the completed documents, together with a certain fee plus two copies of the calendar, to Washington for registration. The forms, with complete instructions, can be obtained by writing to the Register of Copyrights in Washington, D.C., or they can be obtained at any post office. The instructions are clear, and this is something that doesn't require the services of a lawyer.

Incidentally, where can you find patent and trademark lawyers? They are usually listed separately under the "Lawyers" listing in your phone book (and there are not that many of them anyway), or check with your local bar association.

TO SUMMARIZE

Setting up a business requires a good deal of research. You must understand what is involved, and you should never jump in blindly.

You can go to the nearest branch of the Small Business Administration in your area for further guidance on buying a business. (See the Appendix for a listing of its offices.)

Many of the basic forms for uncomplicated arrangements can be obtained commercially or from the court and can be completed without the necessity of a lawyer. *However*, when dealing with matters foreign to you, it is best to acquire the services of legal counsel.

6

Crimes and Other Offenses

You are window shopping on Main Street when suddenly you hear a shout behind you: "That's him. That's the man." You turn to see a policeman approaching, who is accompanied by another person, who is pointing a finger at you. "That's him. I know it." You are being accused of a theft. You are searched and then handcuffed. A squad car pulls up, and off you go to the precinct house.

This type of confrontation is one of the most frightening things that can happen to a person.

During this time, you protest your innocence.

You are taken into the station house and "booked," meaning that your name and the alleged crime are written in a ledger. You are photographed, fingerprinted, and placed in a cell. Depending on where you are, you might be sitting in a "hold tank" among rapists and killers.

What do you do now?

YOUR RIGHTS

First, you have a lawful right to use the telephone. You can make at least two calls, to your family or friends or to an attorney. In some jurisdictions you can make even more, depending on how busy the station house is at the time. If the patrolman who made the arrest was acting in

70

accordance with the law, then immediately after you were arrested you should have been informed of your constitutional rights.

The reading of such rights resulted from the famous 1966 Supreme Court case of *Miranda* v. *Arizona.* Ernesto Miranda was a twenty-three-year-old Mexican with a ninth grade education. A girl had been kidnapped and raped. Miranda was arrested, and after being questioned for two hours he wrote out a confession. He was convicted and sentenced to twenty to thirty years. His appeal went to the Supreme Court, which ruled that the rights of an accused in a criminal case must be protected. It then set forth certain rules for the authorities to follow. These rules are printed on cards that must be shown and read to a suspect upon arrest:

You are under arrest. Before we ask you any questions, you must understand what your rights are.

1. You have a right to remain silent and refuse to answer questions.

2. Anything you do or say may be used against you in a court of law.

3. As we discuss this matter, you have a right to stop answering my questions at any time that you desire.

4. You have the right to a lawyer before speaking to me, to remain silent until you can talk to him, and to have him present during the time you are being questioned.

5. If you desire a lawyer but you cannot afford one, the Public Defender will be provided to you without cost.

6. Do you understand each of these rights as I have explained them to you? Now that I have advised you of your rights, are you willing to answer my questions without an attorney?

Some cards even have a signature space.

Accordingly, before statements can be taken from an arrested suspect and used against him, he must be advised of his constitutional rights, and he must *voluntarily* have waived those rights. If he does not choose to speak to the police after he has been arrested, they can no longer question him.

By another Supreme Court ruling, each state is required to make a lawyer available to every person charged with the commission of a felony or major offense. A federal statute has made public funds available to pay lawyers for all persons accused of a federal offense. Perhaps no other country in the world is so careful to protect the legal rights of persons accused of crimes.

Do you need a lawyer? Several options come into play here. If you are accused of murder in the first degree (which means the premeditated and malicious killing of another human being), it would be advisable to give simply your name and address and to answer no further questions until you have contacted an attorney. However, if the charge is not a serious one, you could tell your story to the police and ask them to corroborate it.

If you can show that you were at a convention, for example, on the day the crime was supposedly committed, and you have witnesses, then by all means tell the police. Their investigation will determine that what you have said is so—or that it isn't. Of course, if your alibi isn't that concrete and you have been charged with a serious crime, you should call an attorney before the *arraignment*.

An arraignment is a procedure in which you are advised by a judge as to the exact nature of the charges against you. You are also informed of your constitutional rights, which include your right to a jury trial and the protection against self-incrimination. At this time you would plead either "Guilty," "Not guilty," or "Not guilty by reason of insanity."

BAIL

At the arraignment the judge will set *bail,* which is the security or monetary guarantee a person charged with a crime must give to assure the court that he will not leave the jurisdiction of the court and will be available when necessary for the trial of the case, or for sentencing after the trial. The purpose of bail is to prevent the accused from being confined to a cell indefinitely while awaiting trail.

To obtain bail you must either post cash or a redeemable bond with the clerk of the court. In almost every jail in the country, the name of your local bailbondsman is listed. The fee for the bailbondsman is usually 10 percent, so if your bail is $1,000, his fee is $100. That fee is not returnable even if you are acquitted. A bonding company charges a premium for a bond, and it will usually not issue one unless the person obtaining it leaves some adequate assurance that there will be no default. In other words, you may have to provide some collateral. A warrant for your arrest will be issued by the court, and the bail will be deemed forfeited if you fail to appear back at the court on the designated date of the trial.

HEARINGS

At the arraignment, assuming that you plead "Not guilty," you can give the judge some facts about your background to indicate that you are of a high moral character. If it is not a capital offense, the judge probably will set either a low bail or permit you to leave on your own recognizance. This means simply that he doesn't consider bail necessary, but you must *promise* to appear in court on the day of the trial or hearing. Remember, the right to bail is not absolute; it depends on the severity of the crime. A judge can deny bail if the prosecution can show that the accused will be a menace to society if released.

The New York City Police Department has been testing a new procedure whereby a citation is issued to a suspect in a minor crime rather than taking him to the station house for booking. This citation is similar to a traffic violation, and when the person signs it, it binds him to appear in court at a later date. In other words, he is making a promise. The police department reports that it has saved considerable amounts of money and countless manhours with this method.

After you have entered your plea and have been permitted to leave on your own recognizance, the next step is the hearing. At this point you hope that the detectives have investigated your story and have found that you were not at the scene of the crime.

Now, suppose the hearing date is set for tomorrow and the detectives haven't completed their report. Is this the time for you to get an attorney? If the case has *not* been dropped after an investigation by the police, or if the investigation has been delayed for whatever reason, you should acquire the services of a competent criminal lawyer. However, if investigation does uncover facts to substantiate that you were not in the city at the time the crime was committed, they will then confront the accuser with this information. But, if the case goes forward to the hearing stage, what happens next?

A *preliminary hearing* is held before a magistrate or a judge. Evidence is submitted by both sides. Your lawyer can be present to examine and cross-examine all witnesses. Certain defenses may be set forth at this time to determine if any constitutional rights have been violated. For instance, suppose you were never apprised of your rights under the *Miranda* decision, or you were not permitted to use the telephone? That could send the case right out the window. If, however, after the proofs and testimonies have been offered and the judge feels there is reasonable and probable cause to detain you, the next step is an *indictment*.

An indictment is an accusation *in writing* that states that a certain person is charged with a designated crime. Webster defines it as "a formal written accusation charging one or more persons with the commission of a crime, presented by a grand jury to the court when the jury has found, after examining the prosecutor's statement of the charge, that there is a valid case."

Indictments are issued only in felony situations. A *felony* is a crime that is punishable by a sentence of more than one year in prison. Its counterpart, the *misdemeanor*, is a crime subject to a prison term of less than one year.

In a felony a grand jury is convened for the purposes of permitting the district attorney to present reasonable cause that a crime has been committed. You cannot be present at such grand jury hearings. If a majority of the jurors finds that there is reasonable cause that you did indeed commit the crime, it will return an indictment, and you must answer for those charges.

Clearly, if you have not obtained an attorney by now, you should do so immediately. And that attorney should be well-versed in criminal law. Calling on a next-door neighbor who specializes in law of the high seas is not appropriate. You want to make sure that you're getting someone expert in the field.

Second, find out how much the lawyer is charging, and on what basis? Is it by the hour? By the week? For defense in a criminal proceeding, a lawyer's fee will depend a great deal on the extent of the crime. $1,000 to defend a felony case is not out of the ordinary. If it is a lump-sum payment, what does it cover? Does it apply to all investigations, hearings, trials, appeals (if any)? All of this should be spelled out in a written agreement. If you do not have sufficient funds to hire an attorney, legal-aid attorneys are usually available. In most courtrooms a public-defender system is on hand to help the indigent. If you can afford an attorney but do not know of a qualified criminal lawyer, call the Bar Referral Service of the local bar association for a recommendation.

Let's assume that the matter is set down for trial. What should you know? Keep in mind that the Constitution affords you the right to a speedy and public trial. This means that you must be tried within a reasonable period of time after the indictment is issued. There are no precise guidelines as to what constitutes a speedy trial. "Reasonable" is the only governing word.

You are also entitled to a trial by jury. This is a constitutional right guaranteed in all criminal cases. Various states have different numbers of jurors who may sit on a criminal matter, but not all states require all jurors to reach a unanimous verdict for conviction, although most do follow that rule. You can also waive your right to a trial by jury. If the jury cannot reach a verdict, it is deemed a *mistrial*, which means that the case either will have to be tried again or it may be dismissed.

You also have the right to confront witnesses. The Sixth Amendment to the Constitution gives the accused the opportunity to examine witnesses and to have the "right of discovery," whereby the names and addresses of all the witnesses the prosecution intends to use may be obtained in advance of the trial. This way the accused can inspect the evidence beforehand. In this case an attorney is essential because this is an extremely technical area of the law.

You have the protection against self-incrimination. This is guaranteed under the Fifth Amendment to the Constitution. It simply means that you cannot be forced to testify against yourself.

To recap, the procedure followed in criminal matters is similar to a train ride. You board at *Arrest*. The first stop is *Arraignment*. The second stop is *Hearing*. The third stop is *Trial*. If you are acquitted at any time along the route, you can disembark the train; otherwise, you just have to stay on until the next station. At which station, though, do you decide whether you really need a lawyer? If you are charged with a serious crime, such as murder, you should obtain one as soon as you get on the train. If you are charged with a crime of considerably less stature, and you have a good alibi, then perhaps you can go to stations One and Two before you have to seek an attorney.

Most people, of course, are not accused of capital crimes. Usually a traffic ticket or some other minor violation is involved, such as smoking in the subway. As an example, try this:

Ellen Evans, twenty-two, is driving home from night school in her 1969 Ford. She is traveling along a major highway at about fifty miles an hour. As she looks into her rear-view mirror, she sees flashing lights behind her. The lights come closer and closer, and she realizes that she is right in the path of a patrol car. Ellen speeds up to pass the vehicles on her right so that she can pull into that lane. When she moves into the right lane to permit the patrol car to pass, she is waved to the side of the road by the patrolman seated on the passenger side. She pulls over. The patrol car stops, the patrolman comes out, and the car continues full tilt down the highway, sirens wailing and lights flashing. The patrolman issues her a speeding ticket.

Ellen Evans appears in traffic court on the date specified. The patrolman takes the stand and says that he had been tracking her car for a good mile and that she was exceeding the speed limit.

At that time, Ellen Evans starts wishing she had a lawyer with her. But, perhaps as will happen to you, she had the best lawyer in the courtroom, namely, the judge.

She takes the stand, is sworn in, and tells the judge her account of what happened.

The judge calls the patrolman to the stand. "Is it your testimony, patrolman, that you were tracking *two* separate vehicles in the *same* lane for one mile and both were exceeding the speed limit?" There is silence, followed by a rap of the gavel. "Case dismissed."

Because this was not a major offense, and the accused told the truth, the judge came to her assistance. In most criminal matters the judge will, in an equitable fashion, come to the aid of the individual who is not represented by counsel to make sure that Constitutional rights are not violated.

ARREST AND SEARCH WARRANTS

Arrest is a frightening experience, even in instances of a simple traffic violation. So, you should know something about the kinds of arrests.

An arrest means a policeman (or even a private citizen) restrains you so that you may be held to answer for a crime or an offense of some sort.

An *arrest warrant* is a document issued by a court. If a policeman says he is acting under the authority of a warrant, he must show it to you and give you an opportunity to read it. A policeman can make an arrest without a warrant if he has reasonable cause to believe that you are committing a felony. He can only make an arrest for a misdemeanor if it is committed in his presence, or with an arrest warrant. If a misdemeanor has not actually been committed in his presence, and he wants to make an arrest, he must ask the court for an arrest warrant.

In order to determine when you need a lawyer, you need to understand the difference between criminal and civil law and the terminology used in criminal law.

Civil law fixes the rights of individuals and defines the protection of their persons and property. In effect, it concerns the relationship of one person to another; thus civil lawsuits are brought by individuals against other individuals, such as actions involving divorces, automobile accidents, adoptions, and contract disputes—anything that is not criminal.

Criminal law, on the other hand, was established to protect society from the harmful acts of an individual; in other words, to maintain peace and order. It concerns the relationship of an individual with his community, whether town, state, or country, and includes crimes such as murder, theft, kidnapping, and treason, and certain less serious crimes, such as disturbing the peace. For the most part, crimes break down into three categories: (1) a felony, where the sentence is for a term of imprisonment for at least one year, (2) a misdemeanor, where the sentence is less than one year but more than fifteen days, and (3) a violation, where the sentence cannot exceed fifteen days in prison. (A traffic infraction is excluded.)

Now, it is embarrassing enough to be arrested by a police officer, but how would you like to be arrested by your neighborhood grocer? The criminal law procedure in the State of New York provides that any person may arrest another for a crime actually committed in his presence. For a felony, it may be anywhere in the state; for a misdemeanor, the arrest can be made only in the county in which it is committed.

The arrest may be made during the day or night, and the arresting party must give the reason for the arrest, unless such factors as resistance or flight make this impossible. Also, one can use only reasonable force in making an arrest when it is necessary to defend himself from immediate physical harm.

And then there is the famous "Knock" rule, where a policeman comes to your door to make an arrest.

"Knock."

He must give you a reasonable period of time to answer.

The only restriction on the knock rule is when the policeman has reasonable cause to believe that (1) his life is in danger, (2) the suspect (you) is escaping, or (3) valuable evidence is being destroyed. If you refuse to let him in, and he has an arrest warrant, then he may break open your door or window to gain entrance. Naturally, he can do this only after he has given you notice of his authority and purpose. In some situations a policeman may stop and detain you by simply placing you under arrest. The law provides that suspicious circumstances be investigated, and thus you could be stopped and asked for certain identification.

The police may also search you for weapons in order to protect themselves from harm. New York, Massachusetts, New Hampshire, Delaware, and Rhode Island, for instance, all have what are known as "stop and frisk" laws. These allow the police to question persons in public places when there is reason to suspect them of having committed, or are about to commit, a crime.

However, in situations where the police have violated your Constitutional rights by excessive force or otherwise, the policeman and the city he works for may be subject to a civil suit by you. Of course, you shouldn't sue the police force and the city without the benefit of legal counsel. If you're going to fight City Hall, then you need ammunition.

Remember this: When you are *lawfully* arrested, you may be searched, and the immediate area of the place of your arrest may be searched. If you are held for questioning by a policeman, and he reasonably suspects that he is in danger, he may search you for weapons or instruments that could cause serious injury. If he finds a dangerous weapon or instrument on you, he may keep it until he finishes the questioning. If he does not arrest you, he must return the item. Naturally he doesn't have to return it if it requires a permit and you don't have that permit. If the policeman, while searching you for dangerous weapons, finds anything that is illegal, he may take it and arrest you for possessing it.

The policeman always needs a warrant to search you *except* where it is incidental to a lawful arrest or under other specific circumstances where the search may be justified by the law.

A *search warrant* is a written order signed by a judge directing a police officer to search a certain place or individual for specific property. The warrant must describe the place or the individual to be searched and what property is being sought. The officer must show you the warrant and give notice of his authority before he begins the search.

Remember, if you are taken into police custody, you have the right to (1) telephone your friends or family in order to notify them of your arrest, (2) speak with a lawyer at the place where you are being held, and (3) remain silent. You can decide to answer some questions or none at all. In fact, before the police can question you, they must advise you of your rights.

As we all know from our Perry Mason days, a defendant (the accused) in a criminal trial is presumed innocent until proven guilty, and the prosecutor has the obligation to prove that guilt beyond a reasonable doubt. If the prosecution fails to establish guilt, it is the duty of the court to dismiss the case. Reasonable doubt has been defined as the doubt that a prudent (or sensible) person can deduce from the evidence presented. You should also be aware that if you are found not guilty or the case is dismissed, you can ask for the return of your fingerprints and photographs, and you can even ask that the record of the case be sealed.

Your right to a lawyer is a fundamental one at every stage of a criminal proceeding. If you appear in court without a lawyer, the judge must allow you a "reasonable time" to obtain one before proceeding. "Reasonable" has been defined as a few days.

Until now *you* have been the accused. But what happens when you are the accuser?

SMALL CRIMINAL COMPLAINTS

Many of us have complaints against others. For example, someone gives you a check for $98 and it bounces. He gives you another check for $98 and that bounces too. Or, how about the upstairs neighbor who plays her eight-track stereo at all hours of the night. You go up to see her.

"I'm your downstairs neighbor, and I was wondering if you could possibly lower your stereo. It's especially difficult trying to sleep with rock music blaring at three in the morning."

"No, I won't."

What do you do?

In many jurisdictions, one part of the criminal court handles nuisance situations and quasi-criminal activities. It's much like the small claims court in civil actions. This rarely used entity (sometimes known as the *small criminal court*) takes care of cases such as small bouncing checks, large barking dogs, and people who disturb the peace. In effect, it pretty much covers those instances where the District Attorney's office cannot take your "problem." As one assistant district attorney said, "We're not a collection agency, and we have plenty of major crimes to handle."

In the case of that upstairs neighbor, you can go to court and fill out a complaint form. Generally, the clerk will help you with it. You don't need a lawyer to do this. You are asking that the court issue a decree that will stop the loud stereo-playing late at night. You get a hearing and you tell it to the judge.

TO SUMMARIZE

The philosophy of this country is that we much prefer to have a hundred guilty people go free than to convict one innocent person. It is not in your best interests to be the exception to that rule. Therefore, use your commonsense knowledge as to when you actually do require the services of an attorney.

It is fascinating to read about the martyrs who perfected the criminal justice system at their own sacrifice. In the 17th century a chap named John Lilburne was brought before the British Star Chamber and accused of printing scandalous books. Lilburne chose not to testify against himself because he felt he was entitled to a fair trial. When Lilburne refused to so testify, he was dragged through the streets of London and then whipped. He still refused to give testimony, so he was then taken to a dungeon and placed in solitary confinement. Still no testimony. He was bound in irons and given nothing to eat or drink. No response. This case led to the protection against self-incrimination and became an integral part of our American system of jurisprudence in the form of the Fifth Amendment.

The decision as to whether or not you need a lawyer in a criminal procedure depends upon the severity of the crime with which you are charged. If the crime is of a serious nature, then immediately obtain the services of an attorney. If you are involved in a lesser crime (a misdemeanor or violation, for example), use your best judgment. But don't be a martyr like Lilburne.

7

Negligence and Malpractice

The American Bar Association survey shows that for every 1,000 adults, 400 are involved in property-damage situations and 120 are involved in personal-injury matters. And the automobile, of course, heads the list. Statistics indicate that roughly 110,000 people are killed in automobile accidents in the United States each year. Despite its advantages, the automobile can be a lethal weapon, and, as such, this sleek piece of machinery is by far the public's prime concern in the areas of personal injury or property damage.

A number of new laws have been enacted and guidelines established regarding these areas, including the "no-fault" law. These laws are so new and the situation so complicated that few people understand the details. One who does is William Alden Wingate, senior partner in the firm of Wingate and Shamis in New York City, who has been a practicing attorney for almost thirty years and is considered to be a leading expert in personal injury and malpractice suits.

In an interview with the authors, he clarified the need for a lawyer in personal-injury and property-damage claims.

THE AUTOMOBILE

Mr. Wingate, has it been your experience that a layman requires the services of an attorney for damage to his car?

Not at all. If a person has been in an accident and has minor property damage to his car and can get an estimate or paid bill as to that damage, there is a good possibility that the other car involved will pay the damage without a lawyer. If the other driver admits responsibility, his estimators will examine the car, look over the bills for the property damage and, hopefully, agree with the appraisal of the damage. They then will offer to pay an amount to fix the car. This can be done without the benefit of counsel.

Of course, if there is no agreement on responsibility or the amount of the damage, then an attorney will be needed.

What about personal injuries?

There are many situations here, too, where a person sustains personal injuries and can handle it himself without retaining legal counsel. The general rule is that if the person sustains *serious* personal injuries, he is better off having somebody else represent him.

There are a number of nuances of law the individual can't handle himself. Only an attorney can best set forth his injuries and get the maximum recovery for him. However, there are instances which arise in the accident field where a person can do without an attorney. For example, in New York State we presently have a "no-fault" law. The first law that was passed became effective on February 1, 1974, but there has been a major change in this law and that went into effect on December 1, 1977. The no-fault law in the State of New York presents situations in which persons do not need counsel.

And this applies to automobile accidents?

Yes. No-fault would not apply to any other kind of accident, such as where a person is injured by a falling ceiling, or by a defective sidewalk, or in a house.

What does "no-fault" mean? Is there a point where the parties cannot sue? In other words, what are the limitations of this law?

Originally, the law passed in 1974 had what was called a $500 threshold to be reached before the injured party could sue for his pain and suffering arising out of an accident. The rule was that unless the injured party sustained at least $500 in hospital bills, doctor bills, dental bills, etc., he could not sue the responsible party for the pain and suffering involved in that particular injury. Of course, if a person was in the hospital for just a few days, he would easily go over that $500 threshold because hospital bills are so large.

That particular no-fault law was in effect from 1974 to 1977. Now it has been changed. The monetary threshold no longer applies. The limit has now become "serious injuries" as described in the law. For example, a fracture or other permanent injury. Thus a person could be injured and spend a week in the hospital and have a $1,000 or $2,000 hospital bill. He then comes out of the hospital fully recovered. If he does *not* sustain a "serious personal injury," as defined under the no-fault statute, he cannot sue for pain and suffering.

Serious injuries today mean (1) an injury that causes some permanent loss of the use of a body organ, member, function, or system, (2) a permanent consequential limitation of the use of a body organ or member, (3) a significant disfigurement, and (4) a fracture. Therefore, regardless of the monetary expense, he cannot sue for pain and suffering under the new no-fault law unless he meets these requirements.

The no-fault law has up to $50,000 worth of benefits that can be paid to a person by his own insurance company. This no-fault category is the largest I can think of in which a person involved in an automobile accident can handle it *without* the services of an attorney. Of course, it goes without saying that if the no-fault carrier involved disputes the reasonableness of the medical bills or the necessity of the medical treatment, then indeed the person needs counsel to collect, even under the provisions of no-fault.

However, if a person has a minor accident and does not have a "serious injury," it is a procedure that he can do by himself. First, he informs his insurance carrier that he has been in an accident and asks that the no-fault forms be mailed to him. Each company that insures a car has to insure the owner of the car and the passengers for no-fault protection under New York State Law.

The carrier's forms have to be filled out. There is a place for the physician's report, a place for the amount of his bills, and a place for the employer to detail how long a person is out of work, including his earnings, etc. The claimant need only complete these forms and send them back to his insurance carrier. Any additional bills and reports that follow can be submitted as they are incurred. The forms themselves should be returned to the carrier as soon as possible.

For example, a person is in an accident and receives emergency treatment at a hospital. X-rays are taken and the results are negative. The person is discharged and advised to see his family physician for a checkup. He goes to that doctor and is told that the injury he sustained is resolved;

in other words, there is no permanent damage. The injured party will find himself with an emergency hospital bill of $60 or $70 and, maybe another $80 for the doctor for three or four visits. He doesn't need an attorney to straighten this out. He submits a bill, his reports, his forms, and under the law he MUST be paid directly by the insurance company within thirty days. If not, he is entitled to interest of two percent per month for any delay in payment.

What happens if the insurance company fails to pay the claim and the individual is forced to hire an attorney?

Under the no-fault law, if the insurance company does not pay within thirty days, the injured party is entitled to two percent per month for such nonpayment. So, there is great incentive on the part of the carriers to make prompt payment.

If the injured party does not receive the money, or if the carrier refuses to accept the medical bills, or if they question the necessity of such medical bills, and as a result the injured party is required to retain an attorney in order to collect the money, then the insurance company must pay the attorney's fees, provided, of course, that the injured party is correct and the company did improperly withhold payment.

The hiring of an attorney at that point will cause the claim to be placed in arbitration under the New York State law. If the arbitrator is satisfied that the medical treatment was caused by the injury—that there was a causal relationship—and that the bills are in a reasonable amount, the arbitrator will then order the insurance company to pay the claimant for his hospital and doctor bills. The arbitrator will also fix the fee for the attorney who was hired to handle that particular arbitration. Sometimes the arbitrator will try to have the insurance company and the attorney agree between themselves as to the proper fee to be paid. The company, of course, pays it.

Under no-fault, in addition to medical bills, hospital bills, medical supplies, and the like, are there any benefits paid as a result of the person being out of work?

Under the no-fault law the insurance company is liable to pay up to $25 a day for all other expenses incurred because of the accident, such as transportation, etc. In addition, if the injured person was employed and can't work because of the injuries sustained in the accident, he can recover from his carrier 80 percent of his wages to a maximum of $1,000 per month. The maximum period is three years. Incidentally, any money recovered from an accident case is income-tax free because it is considered reimbursement for pain and suffering.

If the person is in business for himself and has to hire someone while he is disabled, then he is entitled to recover 80 percent of the money he spends to hire that other person. Again, there is a maximum of $1,000 per month. All of these payments are made upon the proper filing of the necessary papers. I do not think that these papers are so complicated that a person needs an attorney to fill them out.

Understand that I have been talking about the New York State no-fault law. Some states do not have no-fault laws at all. Also, other states that have no-fault have different rules governing them. You must therefore check the law in your own state.

The threshold, as we call it, may be a monetary one, such as $500 or $200 before a victim can sue for pain and suffering. In some states, like New York, the threshold is a definition of "serious injury," and it is limited to certain categories of injuries before a victim can sue. Also, the states that have no-fault laws have varying amounts of benefits that are paid under their respective laws. Moreover, the length of time the benefits run may be different too.

Suppose I own a car and I have it insured, but I am a passenger in another vehicle when we are involved in an accident. Under whose policy do I get the no-fault benefits?

The car in which you are a passenger is primarily liable for up to $50,000 in medical and other expenses, including loss of earnings. The host car is liable, then, under no-fault. If your injuries are such that you are hospitalized for an extended period of time and you use up the no-fault benefits of the host car, then your own car will be secondarily liable under the no-fault law. Your policy then goes into effect, and its coverage is available to you at such time. This, of course, raises many interesting situations, one of which is "excess coverage."

There are many ramifications under the insurance law in which a person should have the benefit of experienced counsel. For example, in one case, a young college student was a passenger in a car being driven by another college student but owned by a third college student. The car went out of control, hit a pole, and the passenger was killed. The owner of the car had only the minimum $10,000/$20,000 New York State insurance, but the operator of that car had coverage under his father's automobile, which was parked in his father's garage. The operator, as a student, was deemed a member of the household under his father's policy. His father had $100,000/$300,000 coverage. So, the deceased's next of kin was able to recover the $10,000 from the coverage of the owner of the car, plus $100,000 more from the insurance company that covered the operator of that vehicle. These are subtleties of the insurance law that make it mandatory to have experienced counsel.

Can you talk about other instances where the layman possibly does not require the services of an attorney?

Two come easily to mind. If a person is riding in the car of a close relative or friend, and the injured party would not want to get a judgment against him above the amount of the insured's policy, then I can see where an attorney might not be needed.

Let's say Ben Smith is riding in his brother John's car. John loses control of the car because he is going too fast on a slippery street, and the car hits a wall. The passenger sustains a fractured leg and is in the hospital for a couple of weeks.

Ben knows by conversation with his brother that there is, unfortunately, only the minimum insurance on the car; let's say, $10,000. The passenger knows, too, that his brother's company agrees that there is negligence, and he knows that his injuries are worth more than $10,000, but he does not want to get a judgment against his brother above the policy.

Ben may not need an attorney because the insurance company, on the issue of good faith, would have no alternative but to offer him the full amount of his brother's coverage. It would be totally unnecessary, in my opinion, for Ben Smith to obtain counsel if he knows only $10,000 is available and he has no intention of seeking more from his brother.

There is another, similar situation. We have here in the State of New York, under the Motor Vehicle Accident Indemnification Law, a maximum recovery of $10,000 per person for a victim of a hit-and-run accident.

What constitutes a hit-and-run accident?

A pedestrian is crossing a street. A car strikes him and knocks him down. The car continues on without stopping. While there are witnesses that the person was hit and struck, no one got the license-plate number. This is a bona fide hit-and-run situation where no one knows the culprit.

Under New York law the person can recover up to the maximum amount of $10,000. If the injuries are clearly worth more than $10,000, it is unnecessary to have an attorney. The state agency (MVAIC) will cover the amount specified. Why pay a fee if the victim will get the same amount anyway? This presupposes no dispute by MVAIC, of course.

There are similar situations. A pedestrian struck by an uninsured car would also be protected under the MVAIC if he does not have a car of his own that provides coverage for him. The MVAIC would pay the maximum $10,000 in coverage per person in the event of an accident with an uninsured car. This is so only in those instances where the victim does not have a car of his own, or he is not a member of a household that has a car covering him as a member of that household. If a person has his own car he has "uninsured motorists" protection as part of his policy.

In the event of a hit-and-run situation or an accident with an uninsured car, his own company would be liable up to the maximum of $10,000 of coverage per person, upon notification of the company and the filing of proper forms.

THE HOME

Suppose I own either a house or an apartment; do I have any special liability to people visiting me?

Certainly. The law with regard to negligence is not limited to the automobile or to the doctor. If a person owns property and if someone sustains an injury as a result of the negligence of the owner, that owner is open to suit by the person who sustained the personal injury.

A case in point; A person digs a well on his farm and covers it up with some light boards. Someone steps on the boards and falls into the well because he was not warned, or the boards were not sufficiently secured. If that person sustains personal injury, the owner can be sued. It can happen in an apartment house too. You have someone up to your apartment, and you know you have a loose rug at the front door. You know that people have slipped on it before, and you haven't fixed it or warned your guest. If he slips, you can be sued.

It is always advisable then that persons owning property have liability insurance to protect them against this kind of occurrence. If a person owns an apartment or a house, he should have liability insurance on that property just as he has insurance on his car. If someone is injured and feels that you are responsible for that injury, he may sue you.

Now, assuming that I own an apartment or lease property and I am sued, what do I do?

Long before you reach the point of being sued by someone, I would suggest that if you know that someone has been injured on your premises, that you immediately report the accident to the insurance carrier or broker. Even the possibility of a claim being made should be reported to the insurance company.

Do I have to hire a lawyer to defend the accident suit?

No. The one who owns the insurance policy is automatically defended by his insurance company. The company hires the lawyer to defend the suit.

Do I have to pay for that attorney if I have an insurance policy?

If you have insurance, the company and its attorneys will protect the suit without any cost to you. However, if you have *inadequate* insurance coverage, your own insurance company may suggest that you retain counsel to defend you above the monetary limits of the policy.

Suppose a person has been injured on my property and agrees to settle within the limits of my policy, but my insurance company refuses to settle with him. What recourse do I have, if any, and should I retain an attorney?

There have been many, many cases on the issue of what is known as "good faith." An insurance company which knows the limits of its client's policy and has good reason to expect that there is liability on the part of the insured and that the verdict may be above the policy, acts in bad faith by not paying the policy.

The company has a duty to relieve its client of the worry and responsibility of a judgment. If it does not, it may very well be liable to you as the homeowner if a judgment is recovered in excess of the policy. In such an event you should retain an attorney to look into the issue of good faith by the company. The law here is well-established: If the insurance company, in "bad faith," does not pay, and as a result the homeowner is saddled with a judgment, the company is liable to that homeowner for that judgment.

We have discussed the person who owns the apartment, home, or property and what rights he has. How about the friendly milkman who trips over a loose board and sustains an injury? When should he obtain an attorney?

A general rule is that if any serious injury is sustained by a person, he should retain legal counsel. If it is a minor injury, the injured party may very well wait to hear from the representative of the homeowner. All insurance companies covering homeowners have claims representatives who will go to see the injured party as soon as the homeowner reports the accident. The representative will interview the injured party, take a statement, and ask for copies of the medical reports and loss of earnings in order to reach a conclusion as to the value of the prospective claim.

However, the claims representatives of the insurance companies are representing their own companies. Their best interests are not with you. If a person retains counsel, it is counsel's duty to try to obtain the best possible recovery for his client. In some instances, if the injury is relatively minor, you can deal with the representative yourself.

If the party is satisfied with the offer that is made, then he doesn't need an attorney. He can receive the check directly. He must be certain, though, that he is not releasing a very serious injury for a small amount of money. He must be aware that he is signing a release that waives all further rights pertaining to the injury. Generally, a person who sustains any serious injury or one who is not certain as to the seriousness of the injury, is better advised to have counsel, and *not* to deal with the claims representative himself.

Incidentally, all jurisdictions have a small claims court. In any instance where the person through the negligence of another sustains injury to his property (such as the cleaner who ruins your coat), he can go to the small claims court in his jurisdiction. The clerk of the court will help him fill out the summons and the complaint. Requirements are spelled out by the clerk, therefore counsel isn't necessary.

This also applies to personal-injury actions that are not covered by no-fault. For example, if a person falls down someone's steps and sprains his ankle because of poor lighting, and feels that a certain sum would adequately compensate him above what is being offered, he can go to small claims court and sue for the particular sum, as long as it is within the limits of that court. He can do this without a lawyer. (The procedure of taking a matter to small claims court is discussed in Chapter 9.)

LEGAL FEES

If an individual, because of the serious nature of the injury or the problems involved with the defendant's insurance company, must hire an attorney to represent him for pain and suffering, could you indicate how the fee structure is worked out. What I am interested in is one of those situations where George and Fay are driving down Lexington Avenue. They stop at 42nd Street. A car hits them in the rear and they are propelled across the intersection. George sustains a fractured leg and Fay sustains another serious injury. They hire the services of an attorney to represent them for these injuries. What is the usual relationship between the client and the attorney as far as fees are concerned?

In New York State we have a contingent fee schedule that is set by the Appellate Division. This governs all attorneys in the state. The attorneys and their clients can agree on different fees provided they are not in excess of the fee schedule handed down by the court. In other words, the fee schedule is the maximum one allowed. The attorney receives 50 percent of the first $1,000 of the sums recovered, 40 percent of the next $2,000, 35 percent of the next $22,000, and 25 percent thereafter. Under the law the attorney's percentage (as based on the fee schedule)

shall be computed on the net sum recovered after deducting taxable costs and disbursements, including expenses for expert medical testimony and investigative or other services properly chargeable to the enforcement of the claim or the prosecution of the action. But, for the following or similar items, there shall be no deduction in computing such percentages: liens, assignments or claims or hospital medical care and treatment by doctors and nurses, or of self-insured or insurance carriers.

This is the exact wording of the contingent-retainer, sliding-scale form used by most attorneys. The fee schedule allows the attorney to reimburse himself first for the actual legal expenses incurred, as permitted by the retainer-agreement, before arriving at the percentage. It also makes it clear that the client is to pay, from his share, all of the liens incurred in the case, such as hospital liens, compensation liens, disability liens, etc., as set forth in the retainer-agreement. (A lien is a claim on the property of another as security against the payment of a debt.)

In addition, the attorney has a right to ask the court for a larger fee than that fixed by the schedule, according to the retainer-agreement.

provided, that in the event extraordinary services are required, you may apply to the court for greater compensation, pursuant to the Special Rules of the Appellate Division regulating the conduct of attorneys.

The client can also agree with the attorney on a straight one-third (33⅓ percent) arrangement at the inception of the case.

MEDICAL MALPRACTICE

What is the definition of medical malpractice?

Medical malpractice is professional negligence practiced by a physician or hospital. It is analogous to a driver who carelessly goes through a red light and hits someone crossing the street. That driver is guilty of automobile negligence. If a doctor needlessly and carelessly harms his patient during treatment, that doctor is guilty of medical malpractice, or negligence.

Malpractice then can be defined as the departure from professional standards of medically accepted practices and care. If the standard and proper practice dictates that a doctor treat a patient in a certain way, and the physician departs from that standard, or treatment, to the detriment of his patient, he has committed malpractice. There is dental malpractice as well. Also, if an attorney does something to the detriment of his client in departing from proper legal practice and care, it is legal malpractice.

Based on your experience, would you suggest the services of an attorney in a malpractice suit?

Definitely. Malpractice in and of itself is not easy to prove. It is well known that physicians hesitate to testify against other physicians on the issue of malpractice. A layperson trying to handle his own case would find this very difficult to overcome. An attorney with experience in the field of malpractice is more likely to receive the assistance of ethical, experienced doctors who are willing to testify against other doctors if malpractice has in fact occurred.

Malpractice cases are highly specialized concerning the measure of legal proof that must be given to the court. Also, the technical wording of the various injuries, the legal procedures, the ability to ascertain that there has in fact been malpractice, are all something that a layperson cannot do by himself. The law governing these cases is extremely difficult to learn.

There are also different statutes and procedural aides to a case that only an attorney can properly avail himself of, such as discovery proceedings, getting court orders to examine hospital records, examinations before trial of the defendant physician, and many other legal aspects. From the technical, substantive, and evidentiary points of view, in a malpractice case, the layperson needs an attorney.

Should the attorney be knowledgeable in the malpractice area?

Yes. And experience in malpractice suits is an important factor. This is not to say that just because a person has handled a lot of cases that he is a better attorney than an attorney who has handled fewer ones. But certainly, the more experience he has, the more he should know and the better he will serve the client.

What's been your experience in the area of wrongful death?

Wrongful death is an extension of the negligence and malpractice law, if, as a result of such negligence or malpractice, the person dies. It could be an immediate death, or it could occur after a period of pain and suffering. The plaintiff would be the executor or administrator of the estate, usually a next of kin, appointed to bring an action.

In a recent case a woman was a passenger on a motorcycle that collided with another vehicle. The plaintiff sustained a broken leg and was taken to the hospital. While she was hospitalized, an action for her personal injuries was instituted. Unfortunately, after eight days the woman was operated on for her broken leg. During the course of that operation, something went wrong. The woman sustained additional serious personal injuries that left her with no cerebral functions whatsoever. Ultimately, she died of the injuries caused by the operation.

The complaint was revised to include an action for wrongful death. We pursued it not only against the doctors but against both vehicles as well. If an automobile accident begins the sequence of events by injuring someone, the negligent automobile operator will be held responsible for all the resulting problems. Here, we had both a personal injury action and a wrongful death action in the same case, as well as automobile negligence and medical malpractice.

If, however, the death of the person was caused by the negligence of the doctors and the hospital involved, isn't it true that the judgment for the death of that person would be solely against them?

No. In fact, if a person's negligence is responsible for a fractured leg, and while that person's leg is being operated on something goes wrong and the victim dies, the automobile driver is responsible not only for the injury of the fractured leg but also for all of the events following the initial injury, as long as there is a causal relationship, even if malpractice subsequently intervenes. The doctors guilty of malpractice are also responsible for the wrongful death.

Would you say, therefore, that in a highly complicated issue of this type, competent counsel would be required to represent the party's interest?

Absolutely. Any wrongful death is certainly above and beyond the ability, in my opinion, of any layperson to handle. Not only is there the technical filing of papers, and appointment of next of kin, or a will to probate, but you need an attorney's experience in evaluating the monetary recovery that would come from such a case. Many cases, laws, and decisions are involved in fixing the maximum amount of recovery usually allowed by the courts in different situations. A highly experienced attorney would be able to get the best possible recovery for a next of kin in a wrongful death action. In other words, because of both technical and substantive problems in a wrongful death, an attorney is essential.

For example, under the law, if a person is killed in an automobile accident, the insurance company for the person who struck the victim would have to pay "death benefits" under no-fault insurance. But in addition to the death benefits, the victim himself may have an automobile parked in his garage and its insurance may contain benefts. The experienced attorney would be able to inform the next of kin of medical and funeral-payment coverage well above the defendant's policy. Some benefits from the usual insurance policy generally are not known to the average person.

TO SUMMARIZE

If you are adequately insured and a claim is made against you, your insurance company will defend your rights. But if you are sued for an amount larger than your insurance provides, you should retain a lawyer.

With certain specific exceptions, a person needs an attorney to represent him in an action for *serious personal injuries.* The exceptions may occur in those instances where the recovery is realistically limited to a small fixed amount. In these situations, it is possible to represent yourself, but an attorney is advisable as soon as any difficulty arises in handling the claim directly.

Malpractice claims against doctors, dentists, hospitals, etc., *always* need the advice and assistance of a competent attorney.

In *undisputed* "no-fault" and small damage claims, generally an attorney is not needed.

8

Wills

They say that to die is the greatest of insults—but it may not be the last. Consider how you'd feel if you knew that because you died intestate or because you drew up your will improperly, there was nothing left for your family by the time your estate was settled. Every state has a different set of regulations for judging the validity of a will, so there are a great many pitfalls you must avoid. Do you realize that if you do not name an executor, the court will—and he'll be paid a hefty fee from your estate? That if a witness to a will is also named *in* the will, it may invalidate the entire thing? That certain kinds of trusts will ensure that an inheritance is subject to taxes only once, rather than several times over? That any typing or printing on a handwritten will or any disposition of property added after your signature may invalidate the entire will?

Does all this mean that you must have a lawyer draw up your will? Not necessarily, but it does mean that you must be absolutely certain of all the regulations governing wills in your particular state and you must comply with all of them if your wishes for the disposition of your property are to be followed.

Let's first define exactly what a will is. A will has no time limit on its effectiveness. Unless it is revoked or amended by a codicil (a supplement to the will), or discharged by a subsequent will, which replaced the first one, you have communicated your intentions.

Consequently every possible contingency must be considered.

Most people think that wills are simple to write, but if you are not aware of the law, many situations could boomerang if you do it yourself. For example, Tom has three daughters: Two live at home, and one lives in another state. Tom is ready to retire. He has saved his money, bought a house with a little property, secured a few stocks and bonds, and has a pension plan. He also has a life insurance policy under which his wife is named as the beneficiary. Tom wants to provide for the future well-being of his family, so he consults with his wife and tells her that he is going to draw a handwritten will, or a *holographic* will. To be valid it must be in the handwriting of the testator (the man who has died), and no typewritten or printed material can appear in the body of the will. It also has to be dated. There is really no need for witnesses, but if there should be, the holographic will may be probated in court as a formal one. (Probate means to have a court formally declare your will valid.) The confusing aspect of a holographic will has to do with its validity. Some states recognize such a will without any witnesses; others accept it only if it conforms to the requirements of the state with respect to witnesses and to the age of the party drawing it up. (See Appendix)

Tom, like most married men, leaves the bulk of his estate to his wife with the proviso that if she dies before he does or if they die simultaneously, all of his property is to be divided equally among his children. However, Tom names only the two daughters who live with him, and not his third daughter. In effect, that daughter is being disinherited.

In a number of states you may disinherit a child, but in this case the intent is questionable. Here the third daughter is simply not named in the will. Did Tom have a lapse of memory? Was it deliberate? Thus, if she decides to make an issue of it, she may be able to convince the court that failure to name her was an *oversight*, and the court could then direct that she be entitled to receive an equal share of the estate with her two sisters. In effect, you may disinherit a child in your will, but you should name that child specifically and indicate that you are in fact disinheriting him or her. Or you can leave that child the sum of "one dollar," which is also considered to be disinheritance. Further, you should set forth the *reasons* why you are excluding a child from receiving a portion of your estate.

This is just one aspect of will-making that shows it's not so simple a procedure. Of course, if Tom had died without leaving a will, the same situation would have arisen. His property would automatically go to his closest heirs. This also means that if his wife had predeceased him, the estate would be divided among his daughters—all *three* of them.

CAUTION: Each state has its own format as to how property may be divided among the heirs; wives and children don't necessarily top the list. Accordingly, you should check the law of your state.

To add insult to injury, if Tom died without a will, the probate court would probably oversee the administration of Tom's property anyway. This means that it would most likely cost his survivors considerably more money to administer an estate without a will.

If there is no will, the court will appoint an administrator who will then marshal all of the assets of the estate, pay funeral expenses and all debts and taxes *out of the estate,* and then will divide the rest to those set forth by the *state* to receive such sums. The administrator also gets paid out of the estate for his efforts, and this can be quite costly.

It is not unusual for an administrator to receive 4 percent on the first $25,000 of the gross estate; 3 percent on the next $75,000; 2 percent on the next $150,000; and 1½ percent on the balance over $250,000.

It is usually the rule for the court to name a close relative or friend as the administrator. And because that person may not be the one you would have chosen, it is best to have a will so that your wishes can be followed.

THE BENEFITS OF A WILL

Many people think that a will is only for those who want to set up trusts or save taxes. Of course, that's true, but the primary reason for making a will is simply to be sure that your property will go to those you care about, and in the proportions you choose.

How do you go about making a will? What must be considered before you do so? What about insurance, estate taxes, children? What are the expenses likely to be of having a will drawn up by a lawyer? What about the terminology? What is probate?

You are said to die *testate* if you have left a will. *Intestate* is dying without a will. The *testator* is the man who leaves a will; the *testatrix* is a woman who leaves a will. *Probate* is the court procedure for officially establishing the validity of a will; in other words, when your will is presented to the court, it is known as "probating the will." The names of the courts that handle estate matters vary from state to state. For example, in California it's the Superior Court, in New York it's the Surrogate Court, while in Pennsylvania it's the Orphans Court.

But what happens if you die without having made a will? It's estimated that as many as one-half of all Americans die without leaving a will. If this happens to you, your property will be distributed among your family members in accordance with the laws of your state, and the distribution may not be in the proportions you would like. For instance, if you are married with one child, your spouse may receive one-half of your estate, with your child getting the other half. If you have more than one child, your spouse may receive one-third of your estate, with the two-thirds divided among your children. It works this way in New York, but it may be different in your jurisdiction, and it may not be what you want. The laws of intestacy are rigid and do not allow for the exception to the rule. For example, if you have a handicapped child, you may want to provide that child with a larger portion of your estate. However, the court cannot give a disproportionate share to that child unless such is stated in a will.

In some states, if your child is under eighteen at the time of your death, the court will appoint a guardian to manage your child's share. Although the court probably would appoint your spouse as guardian, you have no guarantee of this. Thus, if any money had to be used to pay for your child's education, clothing, or living costs, prior approval of the court might be necessary. That could be hard on your spouse. Also, the court would require annual accountings of income and expenses.

Even if you have no children, your spouse still may not receive your entire estate if you die without a will. For example, if your estate exceeds a certain amount, say $25,000, and either or both of your parents are living, then your spouse may receive the $25,000, plus one-half of the balance of your estate. The other half of the estate might go to your parents. You may not want this, particularly if your parents don't need the money. Moreover, you could be forfeiting important tax advantages by leaving the distribution of your estate to the state. And don't forget the hungry federal government and its tax laws.

Remember, a will is tailored to your own particular needs. *You* say who is to receive all your money, and *you* name the *executor* or *executrix*, that is, the party who will watch over the assets of your estate and distribute them in accordance with your instructions. An executor can be a relative, a trusted friend, your lawyer, or even a bank or trust company that specializes in the handling of estates. But the choice of an executor is yours *only if you make a will.*

REQUIREMENTS FOR A VALID WILL

Each state has its own requirements for validating a will in probate court. For example, in most states two witnesses are required. However, there must be three witnesses in Connecticut, Louisiana, Maine, Massachusetts, New Hampshire, South Carolina, and Vermont.

Holographic wills without the signatures of witnesses are not recognized in thirty states. Also, each state has its own minimum-age requirements for a party drawing up a will.

Certain items, such as life-insurance benefits, pensions, or U.S. government savings bonds, cannot be disposed of by a will because you have already designated beneficiaries for them. An exception to the rule governing the proceeds of a life-insurance policy occurs when you name your estate as the beneficiary, in which case the proceeds would be distributed under the terms outlined in your will.

Other assets that you cannot part with by will include jointly owned property with the right of survivorship (it automatically goes to the surviving owner); exempt property (not subject to taxes or governmental regulation), which will go to your spouse and surviving children; and property that you expect to inherit but have not actually received prior to your death.

MAKING A WILL

Before you attempt to make your will, you should know the requirements in your state: Have you reached the required age for disposing of real and personal property? Can you make out a handwritten will? Must there be witnesses? Will it be recognized? (See the Appendix for the requirements in each state.) Your will can be typed, handwritten, or printed, but the form must comply with the laws of your state.

A will should begin with an opening statement as to who you are, that is, your name and address; that you are in control of your faculties and are making the will sanely; and that you are revoking all other wills and codicils that you may have made before. Next, you should provide for the prompt payment of your burial expenses and all debts and taxes. You then provide for the distribution of your estate. If you are leaving anything in trust, that should be spelled out. If you have any minor children, it is best to name a guardian to conduct and handle their business and finances and to care for their general well-being. You should also specify an executor or executrix. You then sign the will, date it, and have the witnesses sign (with their addresses). This is all preceded by a statement by them to the effect that they saw you sign the document, that you stated that it is your will, and that they have signed as witnesses, at your request, in your presence, and in the presence of each other.

But select witnesses carefully because a witness who is needed to prove the will in court *cannot* receive any benefits under it. The intention of the law is to protect you from being *forced* to make a will that benefits someone else. (A sample form of a simple will is included in the Appendix. However, it is included only as an illustration. It may not include vital aspects that would pertain to *your* estate.)

One other point to consider is that it is best to keep the will in a place that is accessible to your executor or family, and tell them where it is. Don't put it in a safe-deposit box because the box could be sealed on your death, and your survivors will have to go through many legal procedures to open it.

Before you draw up a will, you should make a list with the following information:

1. A breakdown of all your assets, including checking and savings accounts, stocks, bonds, interest in money owed to you—everything that translates into cash

2. A breakdown of all real estate held by you anywhere in the world

3. Any obligations, such as debts, liens, or mortgages

4. Any inheritances you may expect to receive before your death

5. Your income and general standard of living during the past few years

6. All insurance

7. Family information, such as the ages and state of health of your spouse and children, adoption papers, marital problems

8. The name of the executor

THE EXECUTOR

It isn't always necessary for a lawyer to act as your executor. Often the executor (male) or executrix (female) is your spouse or a responsible adult child. The executor has the same responsibilities as a court-appointed administrator: He gathers together all the assets, pays all debts and taxes, and distributes the balance to the beneficiaries named under the will. Many times he does this with the help of a lawyer, particularly if the matters are complex.

Executors are entitled to a fee for their services, and these fees are usually set by state laws. Of course, if the executor is a member of your family, that fee could be waived.

If you have named an attorney as the executor to your estate, he may hire another attorney to assist him in the distribution of the assets. But in this case, the estate would be paying two legal fees, perhaps for duplicate work. Therefore, you could include a provision in your will that he *cannot* hire another attorney, or if he does, only one fee (that for the executor) would be paid. In any event, it is always best to provide for a substitute executor in instances where the executor of your first choice cannot serve because of illness, death, change of mind, or any other reason that would prevent him from performing the required duties. The naming of an executor could offset a lot of confusion and possibly legal action.

By now you can see that drawing up a will isn't always easy. Many considerations must be taken into account, and that is why you must plan ahead.

PLANNING YOUR ESTATE

Estate planning can be quite complicated, and you should have an attorney assist you in its preparation. For example, if you have a favorite charity, and you are quite affluent, you could leave it, say, $100,000, with the remainder of your estate going to your husband or wife and children. But suppose at the time you draw your will your estate is valued at 10 million dollars, and suppose you earmarked $9,950,000 for that charity. Further suppose that at the time of your demise your estate is valued at only $50,000. In effect, you have disinherited your wife or husband and children as a result of what may be faulty estate planning. (In many states you cannot exclude your husband or wife from your will; he or she can apply for a portion of your estate through legal proceedings.)

Keep in mind that a will is a document that lives on after you die for a certain period of time; therefore it should be drawn to include as many contingencies as possible. Furthermore, it must be analyzed and updated from time to time to provide for any change of circumstances, not only of your own wealth but also with the responsibility to any other parties. For example, consider the following questions:

* Has the value of your estate gone up or down sufficiently to warrant a revision of the will?
* Has there been a change in the tax laws that would affect the security of your family and dependents?
* Has your marital status changed?
* Has the status of your children or other dependents changed?
* Has the executor or any of your witnesses died?

If the answer to any of these questions is yes, perhaps you should revise your will. In any event, you should review it periodically (about every two years) because the laws affecting wills vary from time to time. You may want to change a clause in the old will or add a codicil, which is a separate document containing the change. There is no limit to the number of codicils that your will can have, but this must be done in writing.

One warning: You cannot rewrite your will by simply scribbling over what has already been written. This would probably void it. In other words, wills are governed by definite formalities that must be observed. For example, a will may become entirely void if any writing disposing of property is included *after* your signature. At the very least, that extra provision would be deemed invalid. In fact, a simple change that was made after you signed or a change that was never initialed could void either that particular change or the entire will.

Do you need an attorney if you want to revise or revoke your will? The answer is that it is best to have one.

ALTERNATIVES TO A WILL

There are alternatives to disposing of your property without the use of a will, and in some situations the services of an attorney are not required. For example, life-insurance benefits are not considered to be part of a person's estate if a certain beneficiary is named. Thus you can take out a large life-insurance policy, name your spouse as beneficiary and your children as substitute beneficiaries in equal shares (in the event your spouse predeceases you or you die simultaneously in an accident), and they will receive the benefits directly.

Insurance proceeds will go into your estate *only* if the estate is specifically named as the beneficiary, or if the person you made as the beneficiary in your insurance policy does not outlive you. However, even though life-insurance benefits go to the beneficiary without the necessity of a court proceeding, they are still subject to the applicability of inheritance-tax laws, depending on how they are set up and the laws in your state.

Do you need an attorney to obtain the proceeds of a life-insurance policy if *you* are the beneficiary? Probably not. All you would have to do is provide the insurance company with a death certificate of the insurer and an affidavit or other documentation to show that you are, in truth, the beneficiary of the policy.

In 1789 Benjamin Franklin wrote: "But in this world nothing can be said to be certain, except death and taxes." And there's hardly a person around who hasn't quoted it since. Enormous tax bites, which continue to increase, are by far the prime concern of most people. However, many have little idea as to what is involved in the way of estate or inheritance taxes. If they knew, they could take precautionary measures while they have the opportunity.

Two basic taxes should be considered: The *federal estate tax*, which your executor pays to the government on the property you own when you die (and this means *all* property, both real and personal), and the *state inheritance tax*. The federal tax is the same whether you live in Maine or Oregon, but you must check your own state regarding the inheritance tax because it varies considerably.

Two aspects of estate tax should concern you: the tax your executor pays on your estate and the tax on estates of persons who share in the proceeds of your estate. Generally if you leave property outright to someone, it will be taxed as part of his estate when he dies. One of the objects in estate planning, then, is to avoid multiple taxes. For example, suppose you leave a large estate to your son. There's a tax on it. Now, the son dies and leaves the rest to *his* son. There's another tax. The grandson dies and leaves it all to his sister. Another tax. But according to the accountants and tax lawyers, if you provide that (1) upon your death the estate is to be held in trust for your son with income payable to him while he is alive, and (2) at his death the trust is to continue for your son's son, and (3) at his death the property would go to the sister, only *one* tax is paid: on *your* death. The other taxes are eliminated.

This is a *trust* arrangement, and it may be the most economical way to avoid a lot of taxes. Also, you can create an irrevocable living trust, where the trustee is instructed to pay all income to you while you are living. Upon your death the principal will be paid to a certain charity. Thus you make only one gift, and that's to a charity—and that's deductible.

The trust is the vehicle most commonly used today in estate planning. It consists of assets that are turned over to a trustee with instructions on how they are to be administered for the benefit of one or more beneficiaries. Depending on the provisions of each particular trust, this method can save taxes, avoid probate, and provide a person with some control over his assets even after death. (Anyone eligible to act as an executor is also eligible to act as a trustee.)

The two types of trusts are *testamentary* (by will) and *living*. A testamentary trust takes effect after death and will not escape probate because it is deemed part of your will. A living trust is established by an individual making a gift of assets to a trustee for the benefit of one or more beneficiaries during his lifetime. Thus the person making the gift can retain some semblance of control over the disposition of his assets. This trust is revocable (it can be revoked at any time) or semirevocable (it may be revoked after a certain length of time or under certain conditions).

You can also establish a trust in which you have no say in the management of the assets after the agreement is drawn. This is an irrevocable trust, and you could be liable for a gift tax. Remember, a trust normally ties up assets for a long period of time. Occasionally it may be advantageous to do this; for instance, where a testator wants to withhold the body of his estate from a child too young to properly handle large sums of money. By the same token, a trust arrangement could provide income for a youngster when he reaches adulthood. Moreover, some trusts give a certain life-estate income to children, with the bulk of the trust going to the grandchildren upon the childrens's death.

But that's not all. Another *commonly used* vehicle for transferring property at death without a will is known as a *Totten Trust* or *bank-account trust*. You simply name a beneficiary to your bank account; the amount of money in the account upon your death will pass to this beneficiary. Although this method is called a trust, you, as the owner of the account, can still deal with your money in any way you see fit during your lifetime. In effect, none of the restrictions or legal obligations applies to the other trusts mentioned above. You can easily make arrangements with your bank for this kind of trust account. A lawyer is *not* necessary. Naturally the formation of more complicated trusts should not be entered into without competent assistance.

Another way of disposing of one's property without a will is by having property held as joint tenancy, meaning that you and your spouse own your house and property jointly. Both names are on the deed. Upon the death of either party, the ownership of the remainder goes to the surviving party without the necessity of a court proceeding. As a matter of good form, the survivor should change the title of the property from the former joint tenancy to the new form.

However, if you live in a community-property state, things could be a little more difficult. In those states it doesn't matter whose name is on the deed. As a result, neither of you can sell the property without the other's consent. But even then differences may arise. In some states all community property goes to the surviving spouse; that is, your spouse becomes the sole owner. In other states the property is divided fifty/fifty between the survivor and your estate. This way you might be able to leave half of your property to someone else. So, even if you live in one of the eight community-property states, you should check the specific law.

Another way to avoid a will is simply to give away all your property before your death. If you want your children to receive your property anyway after you die, there may be no reason to hold it until then.

Federal and state gift taxes should also be considered. These are far less than the inheritance taxes that would have to be paid if the same gift passed through probate. A gift, as part of an estate plan, should be irrevocable (having no strings attached) in order to obtain the largest tax saving.

CHALLENGING A WILL

Assume your uncle dies, and you are unhappy about what he left you in his will. Can you do anything about it? Certainly, if there is a violation of an existing law, you can contest the will on that basis alone. However, let's look at some "different" cases.

After the death of Joe's father, it was discovered that he had left his entire estate to some obscure organization. In this situation, the will might be able to be set aside because it could probably be proved that at the time Joe's father executed it, he did not have the proper mental capacity to appreciate the gravity of his act. The estate was quite sizeable, so Joe hired an attorney to take legal action.

Mary, eighty years old, had been a widow for the past ten years. She drafted a will leaving all of her estate to a man sixty years her junior, thus ignoring her own daughter. The estate is a large one, so obviously the daughter should hire an attorney to determine if the will could be set aside on the grounds that undue influence *may* have been exerted over Mary. It could be that she had been tricked into executing the will or, more importantly, that she had been under the control of one individual to such a degree that her last will was entered into without her being of a free and independent mind. Naturally this would have to be proved, but an objective, experienced lawyer well-versed in this area is the best bet.

A couple lives in California, a community-property state. The husband, at the time of his death, was involved with self-improvement psychiatry and left three-quarters of his estate to an Encounter Group. However, under California law a person who writes a will can dispose of only one-half of his property to anyone or any entity not his or her mate; thus, if he tries to give away more than that, his wife can contest it.

Another couple lives in New Jersey, which is not a community-property state, and the husband does the same thing. Non-community-property states have a "dower and curtesy" law, which in Old English common-law terms means simply that husbands and wives have an interest in each other's separate property at death. With the wife's *right of dower,* she is legally entitled to the use of one-third of her husband's real estate so long as she lives. Some states give the husband a similar right to the real estate of his deceased wife, known as the *right of curtesy.* However, the percentages vary from state to state.

In New York, they are at least one-half of the interest in the other's estate, which means that you can't give away more than that proscribed by the law in violation of the rights of the other. If you do so, the surviving spouse could have the will set aside.

With the exception of your brother's surviving wife, you are the only living relative. Your brother was a good and dutiful husband who left his entire estate to his wife. However, his wife poisoned him. In such a situation, the law provides that if the beneficiary of a will has been convicted of murdering the spouse, he or she cannot collect as a beneficiary of the dead person's will or even under his or her insurance policy.

TO SUMMARIZE

If you are preparing your estate on the basis of a will or a complex trust fund, you should hire the services of an attorney in this area.

Certain steps can be taken whereby an estate can be disposed of prior to death, or even after death, by various legal means. The simplest would be through joint tenancy, life-insurance policies, and the Totten Trust. Upon your death, proceeds from these types of plans would go directly to your survivors.

Because the area of estate planning is complex, the consequences of inadequate planning are treacherous.

By hiring a lawyer to draw up a valid will, you can (1) select the person you want to settle your estate rather than having a stranger appointed by the court; (2) leave your property in trust for your beneficiaries instead of having it all go in a lump sum to certain beneficiaries who can't manage money; and (3) the key point, dispose of your estate in the best way possible for both you and your heirs.

Insofar as costs are concerned, the more complicated the will the higher the fee; however, some lawyers now offer cut-rate services. A $50 fee for drawing up a simple will without a trust, and $150 for a will with a trust, is not unusual.

9

The Courts
and How They Work

In the United States, we have fifty-one court systems: one at the federal level and one for each state. Familiarity with the purpose and structure of courts at each level of the judicial system is important to each of us, whether we encounter legal difficulties, serve on a jury, or never set foot inside a courtroom.

THE FEDERAL COURTS

The U.S. Constitution spells out the condition for a Supreme Court and such others as the Congress sees fit to establish. Under the system established, the federal court system has been divided into circuits. Each circuit has a U.S. Court of Appeals. There are ninety District Courts, with at least one in each state and with some states having as many as four. Other courts have been established for specific purposes: tax court, court of customs, court of claims, court of patents.

Federal courts are responsible for cases under the federal laws. Thus, if you have problems such as federal taxes, patents and treason (to name a choice few), you will find yourself in a federal court.

So as to minimize the number of cases going into a federal court, Congress limited the jurisdiction of these courts (in civil suits especially) to amounts of more than $10,000. Each of the ninety federal district

Federal Court System

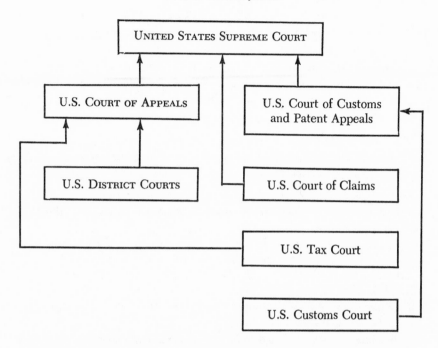

courts is a trial court, so if you were arrested for a federal offense, the case would be heard in a district court in your state. Incidentally, there is one U.S. Court of Appeals in each of the eleven circuits. Most of the cases presented to this court originate in the federal district court within that circuit. Therefore, if you were involved in a federal district court case and felt that there was an error of law committed, you would appeal to the U.S. Court of Appeals.

What is an error of law? It actually means what it says: The court hands down a decision that is clearly against the law. For example, the court might render a decision barring you from instituting a lawsuit on the basis that the statute of limitations has expired, meaning that you didn't commence your lawsuit within a certain period as provided by the statute. The error of law occurs when the court bars you on the basis of such a statute but when you believe that it has misread the law in your particular case. Thus you claim you are entitled to commence the action.

If a decision was rendered against you in the state court, you would appeal to the highest court in your state. If you were still dissatisfied with the results and felt the court had violated federal law or your constitutional rights, you would have the right to appeal to the U.S. Supreme

Court, the highest court in the land. For the most part the Supreme Court handles appeals from the federal system or from a state court system.

However, the Supreme Court may choose not to hear your case. In fact, 90 percent of such requests are refused. Decisions handed down by the Supreme Court are usually considered final, and rarely are they reversed.

THE STATE COURTS

Each state has its own court system, and the jurisdiction of the state courts is usually set forth by state laws. Therefore the cases they handle deal primarily with crimes committed in the state and disputes over ownership of land in the state. Thus, if you wanted to sue a particular party and you were both residents of the state, the courts of your state would have jurisdiction to hear the case. If you were a resident, but the other party was not, you could still sue in that state if the contract or the subject of the suit was under the court's jurisdiction.

The state court system is divided into certain lower courts (such as trial courts) with the higher courts hearing the appeals. Also, many state courts are set up for specific functions; such as juvenile courts, family courts, criminal courts.

A courtroom is divided into two sections, with the audience on one side and the action on the other. These two areas are usually separated by a railing. Generally anyone can go into a courtroom to watch the proceedings. It's free. But in order to be a participant, you must follow certain procedures.

There are a number of ways in which to commence a legal action, depending upon your jurisdiction. The most common is by the service of a *summons* and *complaint*. The summons is simply an indication of who the participants are (that is, the plaintiff and the defendant), the place in which the action will take place (the court), and a brief explanation of the problem. The complaint is a longer version of the problem. It sets forth in detail the particular grievances of the plaintiff. Both documents are then served on the defendant by a process server. In return, the defendant usually serves an answer in response to the allegations of the complaint.

After the summons, complaint, and answer have been served and filed, there are certain proceedings that take place prior to the actual trial.

State and Local Court Systems

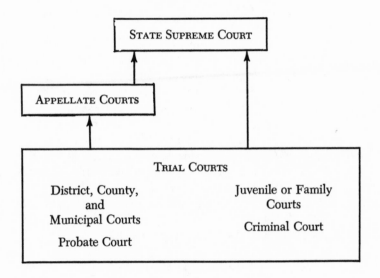

These are known as discovery or pretrial examinations, where one party questions the other (usually through attorneys) to determine the nature of the plaintiff's cause of action and the defendant's defense. They are either oral or written.

The trial is followed by a decision and, depending on the results, the possibility of an appeal to a higher court. Appeals are generally taken on the grounds of errors made in the law that affect the outcome of the case.

There is no doubt that when one is involved in extensive procedures such as this, an attorney is essential. However, in two situations you can dispense with legal representation. One involves the use of the Small Claims Court, the other with arbitration.

SMALL CLAIMS COURT

Small claims court is probably the most underused court system of all, even though almost everyone knows about it. What is not known, however, is that it's *quick, cheap, fair,* and *informal.*

The purpose of small claims court is to handle a case in the shortest possible time, to the satisfaction of all parties. For example, you buy a sheepskin coat for $275. In ten days you have worn it twice and now it has a stain on one sleeve. You take the coat to a cleaner, where it is put into a vat containing a solvent not suitable for sheepskin. The coat is ruined. The cleaner pleads an innocent mistake and offers you $125. You want the full $275. He then offers $175. Apparently that is as much as the insurance company will pay because the coat is now considered to be "used." You hold firm at $275. What happens next?

You have two options: (1) you can accept the offer, or (2) you can sue him.

You decide to sue, but you don't know whether or not you can do it yourself. You call a lawyer and tell him (or her) your story. The lawyer would be happy to represent you, but since small claims court can take up time, usually is held at night, and is some distance from his home, the lawyer quotes you a fee of $100 for his court time. That's a reasonable price, because he might have to sit for hours waiting for the case to be called, or, in the event of a postponement, he may have to come back another night. So, be logical.

Suppose your lawyer is successful and you win the full $275. The cleaner had already made an offer of $175. You pay the lawyer $100, so there's no appreciable gain.

When you take action through small claims court, you are generally on your own. However, before you can sue, certain regulations must be followed.

First, with the exception of criminal matters, most situations involve the sum of $1,000 or less, and they will be civil suits, which means no criminal implications to the procedure.

Although various degrees of complexity exist within the framework of small claims court, the basic procedures are the same in most states. In New York, you can take a claim under the sum of $1,000 into small claims court with specific limitations: Entities such as corporations *cannot* sue in small claims; however they may *be* sued. Also, if you sue a corporation, the defendant *must* be represented by an attorney.

That in and of itself could be an incentive for your opponent to settle. If you find that the cleaner is in fact a corporation, you can sue that entity, and under the law (at least, in New York) the cleaner must appear through an attorney. Thus he may think twice about paying a little more to you rather than possibly a whole lot more to a lawyer. But state laws vary. In Mississippi, for example, if you sue a corporation, the defendant may appear without an attorney.

(See the Appendix for the regulations pertaining to small claims courts in each state. However, one warning: regulations quickly become out-dated, so check with the clerk of the court for more specific or up-to-date information.)

Not every state has what is termed "small claims." Some states, such as Iowa, have conciliation court (which is the equivalent of small claims), while South Carolina has a magistrate's court.

To return to the matter of your sheepskin coat: Attempts to settle with the cleaner are fruitless. He will not budge above $175, and you will not drop beneath $275. You therefore decide to use the services of the small claims court in your jurisdiction.

First, make sure you know who you are suing. Is the cleaner a corporation or a private business? And what is his last name? You can probably determine both by simply looking at his receipt, the signs on his door, in the phone book, or even court records. Business records must be filed with the county clerk's office.

Once you have obtained this information, you can go to the court and ask the clerk how to file your claim. The form usually sets forth a space for your name (since you're the person suing, you are the *plaintiff*), the name of the person you are suing, the *defendant*, the address, the reason for the suit, and the amount you are suing for. The form is simple to complete, but if you have any trouble, ask the clerk to help you. (We have said over and over how helpful clerks of the courts generally are, and it's true.) Give the completed form, and the filing fee (usually a nominal amount, like $4), to the clerk. The court will then arrange to have a summons and complaint served upon the defendant.

Now, there is one element that is extremely important here. The clerk will want to be sure that the small claims court has jurisdiction. Some states allow you to sue a defendant only if he lives within the court's jurisdiction; others may allow a suit only within your district. For example, Washington allows a suit in the district wherein the defendant resides, but Delaware allows you to sue anywhere within that state.

If you have no jurisdiction, then you cannot bring an action in that particular court and you may have to look to another court for redress. For example, if you are suing for copyright infringement, you can sue only in federal court. Therefore it is important that you check the law in your jurisdiction to make sure you qualify for bringing the action into small claims court. Once this is determined, the clerk will prepare a summons and a complaint to the defendant. Usually these documents are combined into one. The clerk will send this to the defendant and advise you of the trial date, which is usually six weeks to two months later, depending upon the congestion of the court calendar.

So, you go home and wait. But within this time you should be preparing your case. First, marshal your evidence. With respect to the sheepskin coat, you'll need:

1. The sales receipt for the coat. This will prove that you bought it ten days before it was ruined in the cleaner's vat. It will also prove what you paid for the coat (you must establish that it cost $275). You can sue for only the actual amount paid unless you are able to attach some "sympathetic" value, i.e., show that its traditional or sentimental.

2. The receipt from the cleaner in order to prove that he received the coat for cleaning.

3. A chronological breakdown of who said what to whom and on what date. Remember, you want to impress upon the court that the cleaner admitted he ruined the coat and that he has already made an offer of $175.

4. If you have witnesses, arrange for them to testify in your behalf.

Your big problem will be in establishing the fact that you wore the coat only twice; that it seems unreasonable for you to lose almost one-third its value in ten-days' time.

The days pass and it is now trial time.

When you arrive at court, the first thing you must check is the calendar, which indicates the cases being held that day. If you're not on the list, tell the clerk.

The calendar will also be read by the court when the judge comes in. When your case is called, stand up and say, "Present." The defendant will also stand up and say, "Present." At this time the judge will ask both you and the defendant if you are ready. But the essence of any defense is delay, so often the defendant will indicate that he is *not* ready, and he may ask for an adjournment or for a "continuance" to another time.

One aspect of being your own lawyer is to proceed with tenacity in order to avoid any meandering and malingering in the proceedings. So, if you are ready for the trial, insist on it. Tell the judge that you're a working person, that you can't afford the luxury of taking too many days off, and that you were never informed by the defendant about an adjournment.

Now, if both sides are ready to go on with the trial, you still may have a few more options to consider. Some jurisdictions offer you the opportunity of either trying your case before the judge (in which event an unfavorable decision rendered to you could be appealed to a higher court), or having the case referred to an arbitrator, usually a lawyer who volunteers to help the court with the caseload. In this situation your case will be heard informally in a private room. The arbitrator will try to work out a settlement between you and the cleaner. An advantage here is that you won't have to wait as long to be heard. The action is immediate. A disadvantage is that in many instances you can't appeal. Therefore, check the law in your jurisdiction. You may not want to forfeit that right of appeal.

Keep in mind that in any civil legal proceeding, the person suing carries the burden of proof and the preponderance of the evidence. What that means in layman's terms is that if there were a scale of justice, the scale must tilt by the weight of the proof, the testimony and the evidence produced by you, the plaintiff. If the scale is even, the defendant will probably prevail (remember, he's innocent until proven guilty), and naturally if it tilts in the defendant's favor, then again, he will prevail.

The format of the trial is a simple one. Both you and the cleaner appear before the judge. You tell your story first. You are sworn in and take the stand to do this. The judge may interrupt to ask you questions. You present your evidence (those receipts) and explain why you should be given judgment for $275.

The defendant, or his counsel, then has the opportunity to cross-examine you. This can be frightening if you are not acquainted with courtroom procedure. But remember, you are simply telling your story, supported by the available documentation of evidence. Be clear. Be concise. Do not be argumentative. Attempt to answer every question truthfully and to the point.

After your testimony, proofs, and the cross-examination is over (this is called the *direct case*), the cleaner may assume his defense by taking the stand. We say *may* because he can also choose to stand mute. Under the law he is not required to take the stand. Assuming that he does, however, he will then present *his* case. He may think that the coat was not worth what you paid for it, or he might even bring in insurance-company statistics showing that goods depreciate a certain percentage as soon as they leave the store . . . much like a car does the instant you drive it off the showroom floor.

When he finishes, you then have the right to cross-examine him, but if you do, make sure that all your questions are directed to the issue at hand. At times, you may have an opportunity to take the stand again in order to rebutt what the defendant has stated.

When the testimony is complete, both sides will usually be allowed to deliver a closing statement. This is a summary of your position: what your case has been, what proof has been shown, and what testimony has been given.

Once this is over, you then wait for the decision. You may get it immediately, or the judge may "reserve" decision, which means he may want to think about it. If that is the case, you will probably receive a notification within a week of the outcome.

If you are successful, a judgment will be entered in your behalf, and the court will then attempt to enforce that judgment by the collection of the money. However, the method of collection varies from state to state. In some jurisdictions, the court does all the work; in others you may have to obtain a *writ of execution,* which you then turn over to a sheriff for collection.

ARBITRATION

Because of the expense of litigation and the crowded court calendars, many persons involved in commercial disputes (shop owners, manufacturers) choose to arbitrate their problems before such tribunals as the American Arbitration Association (known as the AAA, but no connection with the automobile group), which has regional offices throughout the United States. (See the Appendix for the Addresses.) However, both parties must consent to the use of this particular forum.

In effect, an arbitration is a proceeding by which the parties to a controversy, in order to obtain a speedy and inexpensive final disposition of the matter, voluntarily select arbitrators or judges of their own choice and, by consent, submit the dispute to a tribunal rather than a court. Thus arbitration has distinct advantages: it can in many instances diminish the costs for litigation and provide the opportunity to obtain a relatively fast determination of the dispute. In other words, rather than waiting up to three years for your case to be heard in court (if it is not small claims), arbitration proceedings can often be completed within three *months.* Moreover, *immediate arbitration* (within twenty-four hours) is possible when time is important; for instance, if a party cannot proceed with a certain venture without the decision of the arbitration panel. Again, both sides must consent to this forum.

However, the AAA has general rules as to the manner in which an arbitration proceeding is to be conducted. For example, suppose you manufacture outdoor wear, and you have just been given an order for

1,000 blue parkas with fur hoods. You call a furrier for the hoods and send him a purchase order, which he signs. Delivery is to be made within fifteen days. It's a rush job. You prepare the parkas and then wait for the hoods. They don't arrive. You lose the job, and you are left with 1,000 blue parkas. What do you do?

You feel that the furrier is at fault, and you have no intention of spending three years pursuing the matter in court. "There must be a better way," you reason.

And there is. Turn to your signed purchase order and review the small print on the back of the form. Paragraph 24 is an arbitration provision, and it says:

> Any dispute in connection with this purchase order shall be arbitrated in Miami, Florida, pursuant to the rules of the American Arbitration Association and the laws of the State of Florida. Judgment on the arbitration award may be entered in the highest Federal or State court having jurisdiction.

So, you call the AAA to find out the procedure for starting an arbitration hearing.

First, you must give notice to the furrier of your intention to arbitrate. Accordingly, you fill out a *demand form*. This document contains a statement setting forth the nature of the dispute, the amount involved, and the remedies sought. You then send two copies to the regional office of the AAA along with two copies of the purchase order containing the arbitration provision and nominal administrative fee.

The AAA notifies the furrier that you have filed a demand form. He, in turn, can file an answering statement in duplicate with the AAA within seven days after he receives the original notice. (Failure to file an answer does not delay the arbitration.)

Next, the AAA will send you and the furrier a list of arbitrators. You both have the right to select your preferences for an arbitrator, striking from the list any person you do not want. The list will usually include persons who have had some experience in manufacturing, textiles, or clothing, and many will be lawyers.

The tribunal will then designate an arbitrator from that list. If you do not return the list in the specified time, it is assumed that any person selected from the list will be acceptable.

Both parties in the dispute can mutually agree on where the arbitration will be held. If it is not designated within seven days from the date of filing of the demand, the AAA has the authority to determine it, and its decision is final and binding. If a party requests that the hearing be held in a specific locale and the other party files no objection, the locale will be the one requested.

You will then be notified of a hearing date. Like the situation with small claims court, you must begin to marshal the evidence you will need to present before the arbitrator. This includes:

1. The order from the people wanting the parkas
2. The purchase order signed by the furrier
3. Details of what was sent and when
4. Details of the basis on which the order was cancelled
5. Proof of what it cost you to manufacture the parkas
6. Proof of your loss in revenue
7. Testimony of witnesses. (Arrange for them to testify in your behalf at the tribunal.)

Incidentally, whenever more than one arbitrator is involved—and there can be a panel of arbitrators—the decisions of the panel must be by majority rule, unless the concurrence of *all* is expressly required by either the arbitration agreement or by the law of the state in which the hearing is taking place.

The arbitration hearing usually takes place around a table in a closed room. It is an informal gathering; the arbitrator sits at one end of the table, with you and the furrier on either side.

The hearing is opened by filing the oath of the arbitrator, and by recording the place, date, and time. Prior to the beginning of testimony, the arbitrator may ask for opening statements to help clarify the issues involved. As in small claims court, you then present the reasons for your claim, what you intend to prove, and name the witnesses who will testify.

After you have given your testimony, the defending party presents his defense, proof, and witnesses.

The arbitrator, in his discretion, may vary this procedure, but he must afford equal opportunity to all parties for the presentation of any material and relative proof. The arbitrator may ask for additional testimony to clarify his understanding of the matter, and he has the authority to subpoena witnesses, which he may do on his own initiative or at the request of either party. One of the advantages of arbitration is that you can submit affidavits from your witnesses if they are unable to appear. However, the arbitrator may not give affidavits as much weight as he would witnesses. He will also consider any objection made as to the admissibility of such an affidavit.

After the arbitrator has heard and seen all evidence, he then usually has within thirty days to render an award. An award is similar to a judgment, but it does not have legal, binding effect until it is reduced to judgment in a state court. Often, however, the losing party will pay before the judgment is effected.

The appealing aspect of arbitration is its civility. In many instances, you can handle the proceedings without a lawyer. The rules of evidence are greatly relaxed and there is a more casual air than even small claims court. Another plus is the fact that certain proofs that could not be put into a formal court unless foundations were laid, can go into arbitration. Also, in most situations the arbitrators sitting on the tribunal are familiar with the technical aspects of the case. In other words, if it's a textile matter, the arbitrator usually will have knowledge of that area.

TO SUMMARIZE

When you take action in small claims court or through arbitration, you should be well prepared before the trial. Gather your supporting evidence. If you already have a lawyer, certainly tell him what you are doing, and ask if he has any advice.

If you are facing a lawyer representing the person you are suing, the judge will tend to act as yours, particularly if the other side is trying to rely on fairly technical points of law. About 90 percent of the time, the suits filed are settled before they reach trial.

Of course, if the person you are suing doesn't appear, you will automatically win by default.

Don't forget that when the judge starts giving you broad hints (of any sort), he's probably doing you a favor.

Because the stakes in small claims court are relatively low, and because the system is basically on your side, you can usually represent yourself. Remember, the purpose of all courts is to protect your rights individually and as a unit. The court, then, is a common meeting place in which disputes are settled reasonably. According to an American Bar Association survey, 88 percent of the people interviewed felt that if they were accused of a crime, they could expect to get a fair trial; and 77 percent felt that judges were generally honest and fair in deciding each case.

10

Selecting a Lawyer

This chapter will show what a lawyer is, how one becomes a lawyer, the rules of conduct by which he is governed, how he normally charges for his services, what may be expected of him in the representation of a client, and, finally, how one selects a lawyer.

As we noted in the Introduction, we refer to the lawyer as "he" only in the interests of readability. And note that the terms *lawyer* and *attorney* are used interchangeably.

What is a lawyer?

A lawyer is an individual, licensed by the state in which he practices, who gives advice relating to various legal problems. He also drafts documents concerning those rights and, if necessary, represents his client in court in both civil and criminal matters.

Because of the sophisticated demands of our society, the need for lawyers is increasing. Therefore it is important that the person choosing to practice law be responsive to that demand. Accordingly, rather than asking what a lawyer is, the proper question is what *should* a lawyer be?

A lawyer should be a person who is appreciative of his client's problems and the responsibility that society has placed upon him as a member of the legal profession. He *should be* an advocate or champion of a person's rights. He is there to insure and protect his client from any wrongdoing, and if his client has indeed been wronged, he should take the necessary steps to guard the interests of the party he is representing. With this in mind, the various bar associations throughout the country have imposed strict qualifications on the admission of individuals to the practice of law.

How does one become a lawyer?

In most states, in order to become a lawyer, you must have completed a college education and three years of law school (or four, if you attend at night). After that comes a rigid bar examination. In addition, there is a screening process before a Character and Fitness Committee, the purpose being to examine your background in order to determine whether or not you have encountered any legal "troubles" during your lifetime. In effect, this committee decides whether or not you are capable to accept the responsibilities of being a practicing attorney.

The road to admission to the bar is long, tedious, and difficult. Those aspiring to the legal profession should be of the highest caliber because they are involved not only with the civil rights of individuals but with protecting the basic freedoms upon which the law is based.

Upon the completion of these studies and after passing the entrance examination, a lawyer might decide to specialize in a particular area, such as criminal law, copyrights, or real estate.

For the most part law schools teach standard courses in the areas an attorney will encounter in private practice:

* Criminal law, which includes substantive and procedural aspects of criminal proceedings for both prosecution and the defense.
* Constitutional law, which is the basis of all law in this country.
* Torts, which include accident cases and negligence actions.
* Wills, which includes not only the drawing up of wills but also litigation that arises in will-contest matters, plus other situations, including probate proceedings.
* Corporations and partnerships, which includes how one forms same, what are the necessary ingredients to the formation of a business entity and again, the litigation that is involved.
* Other courses such as maritime law, labor law, administrative law, domestic relations, and real-estate law.

Extra curricular programs also assist the law student in the pursuit of his profession. These include Moot Court, a system whereby students actually try fictitious lawsuits in order to gain experience in gathering evidence, preparing, examining, and cross-examining witnesses, and "summing up" to a jury.

In addition, programs are offered under the heading "Law Review," an arrangement whereby the top law students prepare articles requiring extensive research in various areas of the law. The articles eventually are published in a document or periodical called a *Law Review*.

When the student finishes his formal education at a law school, he usually attends what is called a Bar Review Preparatory Course, which is a review of all three years' study. The bar examination given by the various states in which the candidate chooses to practice is a series of comprehensive questions (usually given over a two-day period) covering the entire field of study. If the candidate is successful (and in many states, the rate of success is moderate to low), he is interviewed by the Character and Fitness Committee as to whether or not he is suitable for the practice of law. Assuming that he is, he is sworn in by the judge of the state's highest court and receives a license to "hang out his shingle."

Of course, it's one thing to have successfully completed three years of academic studies and to have taken the bar exam, but it's another to deal with a real, live client. Therefore many people coming out of law school decide not to hang out that shingle, and instead they enter governmental bureaus or administrative agencies in their field. This is often a wise decision, for it gives them practical experience in the everyday world. A few years' work in the District Attorney's office is most beneficial prior to entering private practice and specializing in criminal law.

However, any new attorney must adhere to the rigid rules of conduct in his practice.

What are these regulations?

The American Bar Association has set forth a Code of Professional Responsibilities that each attorney must follow in the practice of law. These rules are called Canons, and understanding them will be helpful to a layperson in dealing with an attorney.

CANONS OF ETHICS

Canon #1

A lawyer should assist in maintaining the integrity and competence of the legal profession. This means that each lawyer is charged with keeping the practice of law honest and at a high capability level.

Canon #2

A lawyer should assist the legal profession in fulfilling its duty to make legal counsel available. This canon supports the proposition that all citizens are entitled to equal protection under the American system of law. Thus, in order to insure the protection of an individual's rights, competent legal counsel should be available to each citizen.

Canon #3

A lawyer should assist in preventing the unauthorized practice of law. This section concerns curbstone lawyers. The neighborhood barber who renders legal advice may be harmless. But when those in positions of power—accountants or bank officers or other individuals in areas of trust—overstep their bounds and dispense legal opinions without the necessary training, they should be discouraged. In order to prevent unauthorized and dangerous situations of this type, steps may be taken by the proper authorities (such as the bar associations) in order to protect the public from being harmed by such individuals.

Canon #4

A lawyer should preserve the confidences of a client. This is one of the most important functions of an attorney, and also relates historically to the privileges rendered to those who practice medicine or are in the religious field.

A client cannot have confidence in an attorney who reveals the client's deepest secrets to others. A shield law protects the interests and confidences of clients, and no attorney is forced to reveal what has been supplied to him by his client even in a court of law. There are certain exceptions to this rule, but primarily information related to the attorney is considered privileged and cannot be released without the client's approval. Revealing privileged information would essentially subvert the entire concept of legal justice in this country.

Canon #5

A lawyer should exercise independent professional judgment. This simply means that if a man arrested for allegedly molesting a three-year-old is receiving the scorn, ridicule, and hatred of the community, the attorney is charged with the responsibility of disassociating himself from the claims and pressures of society in order to make his own independent professional judgment as to the protection of his client's interests.

Canon #6

A lawyer should represent a client competently. Although this is understood—and one would think it would be understood in the practice of any profession—the bar associations have chosen to set forth this canon explicitly to reinforce in the minds of attorneys (and the public) that an attorney must use all of his professional skills and diligence in the representation of his client.

Canon #7

A lawyer should represent a client zealously *within the bounds of law.* This is a very important canon and one the layman should understand completely.

An attorney should never be required to manufacture evidence or to withhold evidence that has been called for or to prepare witnesses to testify to matters that really did not occur. This is not only unfair to the attorney (and the attorney should be censured or disbarred for doing this), but it is totally against the best interests of the client. Playing outside of the rules usually leads to disaster not only for the attorney but for the client as well.

Obviously some individuals have committed "crimes" and have then been set free by the courts. Unfortunately this happens. But just as the attorneys are bound by rules of conduct, the entire course of a legal proceeding is governed by certain rules too. In criminal actions, for example, every person is presumed to be innocent until proven guilty. The prosecutor is charged with the duty of setting forth his case and proving his case with a preponderance of the evidence tilted in behalf of the prosecution.

By the same token, even a defense lawyer (who knows in his heart that his client is guilty) is charged by the oath he has taken to make sure that the client is not railroaded and that the prosecutor (and court) play by the rules set up by the Constitution. If the prosecution fails within the rules set forth, that client will usually go free. Bear in mind that it is not because the attorney who has defended that individual has not played by the rules but rather that the weight of evidence as presented by the prosecution was insufficient in order to convict. In many acquittals, therefore, the defense has not necessarily won; the prosecution has lost.

Canon #8

A lawyer should assist in improving the legal system. This means that the lawyer should always be aware of the ways in which the system can be updated in order to protect the interests of all citizens. He must use his best efforts to improve the present structure in furtherance of this concept.

Canon #9

A lawyer should avoid the appearance of impropriety. An attorney is charged with the responsibility of conducting his life in a manner so as not to degrade or reduce the seriousness of the practice of law in any respect. This does not mean that he cannot wear a lampshade at parties, but that his method of operation should not place him in a position where it could be misunderstood with respect to his client and the profession as a whole.

Other "don'ts," too, are placed upon the attorney in the practice of law. For example, attorneys cannot solicit clients by unprofessional or illegal means. This is the so-called ambulance-chasing concept, and the scenario may be familiar.

You are driving down Main Street when, as you cross the intersection of Elm, a driver goes through a stop sign, hits your car, forcing it onto the sidewalk. Fortunately, no serious injuries result, but your car is a total wreck and must be towed away. The police arrive, and you make a phone call to the nearest tow-truck operator. In minutes he pulls up. While he looks over your car, he tells you about a lawyer-friend of his. He also gives you the lawyer's card and tells you he can be reached any hour of the day or night. In many instances, that lawyer pays the tow-truck operator a kickback for referring injury cases to him. This is illegal and dangerous, not only to the legal profession but to the public. The tow-truck operator is not interested in the qualifications of the lawyer, but in the size of his kickback. Therefore he may be referring you to an attorney whose credentials are not best for your problem.

Illegal kickbacks and references apply not only to tow-truck operators but to hospital nurses or attendants, or even doctors. In fact, in certain communities, it has been found that policemen, ambulance drivers, and insurance agents have been involved in illegal setups of this type.

It is often difficult in a time of anxiety and upset to fend off such heavy-handed practices when you are not in a position to protect your own interests. The only thing you can do is to be aware that it exists. It is disconcerting to wake up in a hospital room with people peering over you, especially when one of them is an attorney who shoves a contingent-retainer agreement in your face and asks you to "sign up" so he can represent you.

Other situations you want to avoid are those where an attorney takes your money or property and places same in a pot with others—or his own money. There should be no comingling of funds. Even though there may be no wrongdoing or wrong-intent, the ABA has promulgated a rule to prevent such practices.

If any of these situations happen to you, contact the local bar association for proper action to be taken against the offending party. The intention should always be to stop these degrading and illegal procedures from taking place—both now and in the future.

How should you select a lawyer?

It has been said that if people spent as much time selecting their lawyers as they spend picking out their new automobiles, the legal profession would have few public-relations problems. Research shows that half of the public selects a lawyer on the recommendation of someone other than the client's prior lawyer; that is, a friend or relative. And a third of the remaining half knows the lawyer personally, but in another context—perhaps as a member of a club, or one who lives across the hall or works out in the same gym. The rest are sought through bar associations, legal aid societies, and the phone book.

Before selecting your lawyer, you have to understand what type of lawyer you need. This is an age of specialization, and, like the medical profession, there is little general practice. Most lawyers limit themselves to certain areas; thus you must be extremely cautious that you retain someone who knows the area of your problem. Practically all lawyers have a smattering of every area of the law from their law school days, but the technical expertise required to practice in a particular area more often takes on-the-job training. Thus, if you need a lawyer to handle a criminal matter, you may not be in the best of hands with a lawyer whose practice is primarily estate planning. (Of course, should you be convicted and put away for a goodly number of years, then that estate lawyer may indeed come in handy.)

One sidelight: Who actually uses lawyers, and in what areas? Again, back to that ABA survey, which found that 71 percent of the people interviewed acquired real property, but oddly enough only 39 percent consulted a lawyer. In job-discrimination problems, only 1 percent consulted a lawyer, while 69 percent did so in divorce proceedings. And 85 percent sought lawyers in estate planning, particularly in the preparation of wills. This means that the highest proportion of lawyer-use was a fat 790 consultations per 1,000 people in the area of estate planning. With marital problems the figure was 670 consultations per 1,000, while real property had 370 consultations per 1,000. The lowest? Employment matters, with 40 consultations per 1,000. Thus wills had the highest usage, and this means that the types of problems generally taken to lawyers are: (1) estate planning (wills), (2) marital matters, and (3) real property.

Sooner or later, almost everyone needs a lawyer. Many people, of course, think of seeing one only *after* they get into trouble. The best time to consult an attorney is obviously before you have that legal problem. Prevention is still the best bet.

Now, what else should you keep in mind when selecting a lawyer? Common sense and a little bit of investigation are the rules here. If you have a common cold, you go to a general practitioner; if you have a serious heart ailment you go to a cardiologist. But if you go to a general practitioner with a heart ailment, he will, in good conscience, refer you to a specialist.

In the legal field, there is a slight twist: You may have to diagnose your own problem. For example, if you are drawing up simple will, handling a simple traffic violation, or preparing for an uncomplicated closing on a house, a general practitioner is surely competent to handle it. But if you have a knotty problem, such as the state is about to condemn your property, or you have written a manuscript you would like produced on Broadway, or you have perfected a new can opener and want to patent it, then it may be in your best interests to seek the services of a specialist.

If you do not know of an attorney who handles uncomplicated matters, you can ask a neighbor or friend who may have used an attorney's services. Ask them if they were pleased with what the attorney had done and if the fee charged was fair and equitable.

In this society nearly everyone must use the services of an attorney at one time or another. Of course, it is not sufficient merely to obtain the name and address of a lawyer; you must attempt to find out if the lawyer has dealt with a problem similar to or the same as yours.

THE TYPES OF LAWYERS

Lawyers fall into various categories: Some work in the civil field, some in the criminal field. A number may be specialists in one field. For example, a civil attorney is not necessarily a copyright lawyer or involved in the day-to-day activities in the formation and operation of a partnership.

If you cannot find the name and address of an attorney through a close friend, relative, or business associate, contact your local bar association. It has referral services and will give you the name of an attorney who, for a very low fee, will meet with you and help to determine what type of services you need.

Once you have received the name and address of an attorney and have called to set up an appointment, you now must consider everything you see and hear when you meet with him. Lawyers come from various backgrounds, and the diplomas on the wall do not guarantee that you are getting the best for you. Sometimes those from the most prestigious law schools leave something to be desired, while those from rather obscure schools handle your particular problem well. Or, as one lawyer said, "Some of the best people graduated from schools you never heard of, and some of the worst have a lot of fancy degrees."

So, look carefully at what is on that wall. See whether or not there are any recognitions from any society or bar association groups that may indicate that the attorney is a specialist in a particular area. For instance, if you have a real estate problem, check to see whether or not he has received any special verification from a real-estate society or even from the real-estate group of a bar association.

Remember, too, that many lawyers are specialists *not* in a part of the law but rather in an industry. Thus a lawyer for the Meat Cutters Association may know everything there is to know about unions, but he may not be able to handle a lawsuit against the local butcher who sold you bad meat.

Ask the lawyer about his experience and expertise in the area of your problem. Any lawyer worth his salt, and knowing the anxiety of a client, will have no qualms about dealing with questions referring to his qualifications. Remember, you need someone who is not only interested in you but who can meet your needs.

In situations where your personal liberty may be at stake (such as in criminal actions), ask the attorney if he has handled such matters before. What's his background in that area? Has he had any prosecuting experience? Ask him about his track record with respect to the crime in which you are involved. Was he successful; if not, why not?

It is dismaying that people spend more time comparison-shopping for a refrigerator than for an attorney or a physician. Many times a person will simply take the recommendation of his local grocer, thus possibly throwing his reputation, money, and liberty into the hands of an individual who he has not checked out.

Perhaps some of the best representation is offered to those who cannot afford an attorney. For those who have been charged with a crime and cannot ante up the money for a lawyer, there are legal aid societies (or public defender offices) in most jurisdictions. A lawyer will then be assigned.

Most legal-aid lawyers come from local law schools as a first job, although some come from government agencies, and a few enter the legal-aid area from private practice because they would rather do something they really believed in. Legal-aid staffs are energetic, devoted people who have some familiarity with the problems involved—in fact, many times to a greater degree than other general practitioners in the same community.

Then there is the "store-front" lawyer, who has set up an inexpensive office in a modest-incomes neighborhood. His rates are low, and the quality of service is generally sufficient for everyday problems.

Also group-insurance plans now provide legal services in certain parts of the country. About two million American families are presently enrolled in prepaid legal plans that are not too dissimilar from the medical group-insurance plans. In other words, the employee and employer of a company each contribute a nominal amount every week (like $1) to a group plan underwritten by an insurance company and sponsored by a state bar association. The plan offers a full range of services, from wills to divorces to house problems.

For the very rich, of course, there is no problem; they can hire the best legal counsel in the country to handle their traffic tickets. But middle-class citizens in this country can neither afford the "best," nor can they be supplied free, competent legal help. The burden, therefore, is left upon their shoulders, and they must handle their own legal problems by selecting—and being able to afford—the most qualified counsel they can find.

Again, if you do require the services of a specialist and do have a general attorney, that attorney should be able to provide you with names of specialists in the area you need.

Suppose you are that one individual with the unpublished Broadway play. What you need, then, is an attorney who specializes in the entertainment field. This field includes motion pictures, television, theater, radio,newspapers, books, and night clubs, and it is peculiar unto itself. For example, Robert Youdelman, an attorney in New York City with more than twenty years experience in all branches of the entertainment field, has been counsel at a large theatrical agency. He has also been an agent and has been an attorney to writers, producers, performers, and directors.

According to Mr. Youdelman, many problems arise on contracts where the lawyer wasn't consulted before it was signed. He says that the entertainment business has a "high gloss of friendship," and that when it comes to signing a contract "no one wants to do anything to offend his new friend and risk losing the big chance. Thus they may not seek counsel."

What he is referring to, of course, is the new entry into the field: the budding writer, the first-time producer, the new chorus girl.

"This is a highly specialized area of the law," says Mr. Youdelman. "There are not that many of us who work in this field full time. Perhaps that's why most of us are either in New York or Los Angeles. That's where the business primarily is." Now, suppose you are that budding author, and you live in Oxford, Mississippi? "We can handle the guy in Mississippi," says Mr. Youdelman. "Most of our business is done on the phone anyway. Distance doesn't hamper it." So how do you find a lawyer like Bob Youdelman? "Most of the theatrical lawyers are known by the various unions and guilds. You can call the Dramatists Guild, the Authors Guild, AFTRA, or SAG and get a slew of names. Various university workshops know of theatrical lawyers too."

Do you need an attorney? According to Mr. Youdelman, having a knowledgeable attorney will never hurt you in a deal with responsible people.

"Take the writer. He feels lucky to have a publisher. So, he considers it not worthwhile for him to get a lawyer. If the writer believes in himself and what he writes, he should really protect himself. Does he know what he is giving away? You must protect the areas up front and not underestimate the long range value of what you are doing. When it comes to signing your name to a piece of paper, call an experienced lawyer. But, remember, get somebody who *knows* the field."

That's the key, and it applies to any area of the law. Don't hesitate to call upon your family attorney or local practitioner (even if you have never dealt with him before) to assist you in the selection of a specialist if you need one. The best of all possible worlds, of course, is to find an attorney who is not only competent to handle your problem but also is one whom you can trust. Bedside manner is not exclusively within the domain of doctors. It is also within the domain of the lawyer. You should find an individual you can relate to. Remember, make your selection of an attorney based upon his credentials and his competence, not on the quality of the furniture in his waiting room.

LEGAL FEES

Abraham Lincoln was once quoted as saying that "a lawyer's time and advice is his stock in trade." Probably the most basic ingredient in any fee charged by a lawyer is the time spent on a particular problem. A lawyer's professional services differ from those of a doctor or dentist in one important way: Much of the work is done when the client is not present. Therefore many people are unaware that the four-page document drawn up for them, or the advice given in a few minutes on the phone, is actually the result of many hours of research, and that research may also have involved a legal assistant, a lawyer associate, and a legal secretary. Keep in mind that when you engage the services of an attorney, you are really hiring the entire law office to work for you—at least in most cases, depending on the particular problem.

In large cities big law partnerships exist with experts in most fields. Thus, if the partner you originally contacted is the wrong one, he will provide an appropriate person within his partnership. Smaller firms, on the other hand, usually maintain similar relationships with outside experts in specialties that they themselves do not handle.

An attorney has nothing to sell but time and advice. He doesn't peddle soap, ties, hamburgers, or frozen yogurt. For his time and advice, he charges, and it is generally in three ways:

1. *Flat Fee:* A client approaches an attorney on a rather simple matter, such as drawing up a will, drafting a contract, or representation for a real estate purchase. The attorney will usually indicate at the first consultation what it will cost. He will quote a flat sum for the services to be rendered. Should the work, for any reason, go beyond the drafting of the particular document—because the client requested changes or because of subsequent, unforeseen events, then an additional fee may be charged.

Nevertheless it is in the best interests of everyone involved (including the attorney) that the fee is clearly understood by all parties. If the attorney is charging $100 to draw a will but another $25 to file it in certain jurisdictions (for whatever reason), then it should be so stated.

Generally, when an attorney deals with a client the first time, he sets forth a fee-retainer agreement. This is simply an agreement whereby the duty to be performed by the attorney and the fee for his services are spelled out. It can be in the form of a letter, and it is certainly not complicated.

Of course, if an attorney and a client have had an ongoing and long-term relationship where they have understood one another for many years, sometimes a handshake is sufficient to finalize the arrangement on what is to be done and the fee that is to be paid. This does not suggest, however, that this is the best method for either the attorney or the client. It is always better to clarify the agreement in a memorandum of some sort, which each of the parties signs.

Many times, in addition to the regular fees, certain disbursements and expenses must be considered. There are usually monies the attorney has paid out of his own pocket on behalf of his client. They cover court costs, investigators' fees, deposition fees. In other words, if you are involved in a matrimonial matter, you will pay the lawyer what he has expended in the way of costs for filing the papers in court, various statements that may have had to be obtained from certain interested parties, and the charges levied by administrative bodies with respect to the work he is doing.

In addition, because of the inflationary spiral today, the cost of practicing law has gone up considerably. In the past most lawyers absorbed such costs as postage, photocopying, phone calls, messenger services. Now they are passing them on to the client. Therefore it is necessary to approximate what costs may be incurred on top of the flat fee. Ask the lawyer what reasonable expenses he will be absorbing with respect to the particular work he is doing for you. You can also place a limit, or ceiling, on such expenses. For example, you will pay for expenses up to $50; anything above that must be approved by you before the attorney may incur them. You don't want to pay $100 for him to draw a will and then, for some strange reason, be on the hook for $200 in costs. Again, this should all be put in writing.

2. *By the Hour:* The fees for hourly rates can be anywhere from $10 to who-knows-what, depending on the specialty involved. However, assume that an attorney is involved in representing a client in a complex tax situation, and because of certain problems, there is no way to tell how much time or effort will be necessary in order to bring the matter to a successful conclusion. Of course, you can opt for a flat fee, but consider this: Suppose the attorney agrees to charge you $500 for the work he has to do, and suppose it takes him exactly forty-seven minutes to solve the

problem. On the other hand, suppose he has to expend forty-five hours reaching the conclusion. The attorney then has to compute what to charge based on his feeling of what kind of services he will have to render and over what period of time. Therefore many lawyers will charge an advance retainer against an hourly rate.

What this means is that the attorney will figure that it will take him ten hours to complete the work, and at $50 an hour it comes to $500. So, he will charge an advance of $500 against $50 an hour. When he uses up the ten hours, then the per-hour fee goes into effect. The advance then is applied to the subsequent hours involved by the attorney in the pursuit of his client's problem.

What kind of hourly rates exist? They range all over the lot; however, a client could be expected to pay a higher rate for those attorneys who are involved in specialties of the law because of their expertise. Lawyers practicing specialties will generally charge higher fees than the general practitioner. We know this from the medical profession: The urologist will usually charge more for his time than will the regular GP.

Lawyers who charge an hourly rate are supposed to keep *time sheets*. These indicate what work has been done for the client, on what date, and how much time was involved. A client is entitled to see his time sheet.

Don't forget that sometimes what's cheap is dear. Therefore if you choose to retain the services of an attorney in a highly complex area of the law who has little or no expertise, you may ultimately pay him more: as a result of a possible unsuccessful piece of litigation or in the way of receiving less monies because of the lawyer's inability to deal with the matter on as high a professional level as a specialist would. Also, some attorneys will charge a per-day rate for a court appearance. For example, $100 a day to appear for you in a local court to $300 per day to appear in a superior or higher court.

3. *Contingencies:* Contingency is a fee arrangement whereby the lawyer receives a percentage of the sums recovered for his efforts on behalf of the client. This is mostly seen in accident cases where personal injuries are involved: in an automobile accident or simply from tripping in a pothole and breaking a leg. A contingent fee may be employed in other situations too: where the client cannot afford the costs of litigation or the attorney's per-hour fee and therefore indicates to the attorney that he would permit the lawyer to share in the successful completion of the case.

Many states have set forth what is known as a "sliding scale" schedule for attorneys to use in connection with personal-injury cases. Generally these fees do approach approximately one-third of the sums recovered, but in some states the fee may be higher. Each state can have its own sliding-scale arrangement.

Contingent fees have been the object of much criticism. Many feel it is an unfair arrangement, claiming that the attorney gets too much and the client too little.

However, look at it this way: Many times, the poor cannot afford the services of an attorney in certain personal-injury actions, and the only way they can acquire proper legal representation, of both the general practitioner and the specialist, is through the contingent-fee arrangement.

No doubt, unfair situations exist. For example, a person in an automobile accident sustains medical charges of $5,000. He learns that the defendant has a $10,000 policy and no other assets to speak of. If the attorney is on a one-third basis, he will then receive $3,333.33, plus costs and disbursements. Considering that the medical charges were $5,000, the client is left with a little more than $1,500 for the injuries he sustained.

This is why a person may not need the services of an attorney. In such an instance, it may be possible for the injured party to collect the full $10,000 of the insurance policy, and thus with the deduction of the $5,000 for medical charges, he is left with $5,000; certainly more than the $1,500 when the lawyer was involved.

Incidentally, many states regulate attorneys' fees where children are concerned. In the case of a child under the legal age, the fees to be charged by the attorney must be approved by the court *prior* to any settlement arrangement. You might want to check the laws of your state on this aspect.

In order to further understand how contingent-fee arrangements are made, consider the following example: Assume that you have tripped over some cracked concrete and have been injured. You hire an attorney on the basis of his receiving one-third of the sums he recovers. You have received $700 in medical and hospital bills as a result of your injury. Your attorney sues the negligent party, and the case is eventually settled for the sum of $6,500. The attorney has expended the sum of $500 for court costs, investigator's fees, photocopying of hospital records, doctors' reports, and the like.

The mathematics would be as follows:

Total Settlement:	$6,500
Attorney's expenses:	− 500
Net Sum:	$6,000

Attorney's fee based on one-third is: $2,000 (He receives it on the net sum of $6,000, not on the settlement sum of $6,500; he's just had his expenses taken off the top.) Your check: $4,000

Remember, you absorbed the cost of your own medical treatment, which amounted to $700. Needless to say, there are many insurance policies that would pay for that $700, but if you have not been reimbursed, then you have really netted some $3,300.

What happens if you lose the case? Obviously you would collect nothing, and the attorney would collect the same. But what about expenses? Are you liable for out-of-pocket expenses incurred by the attorney: court costs, photocopying, telephone calls? Technically the client is supposed to pay for these, but in practice most lawyers absorb these sums as the expense of doing business.

A contingent-fee arrangement should be set forth in an agreement between you and the attorney so that there is no question of who is to receive what. Since many contingent fees in accident cases are regulated by the state, the state may also supply the form to be filled out. (Accordingly, the attorney can use only those documents so recognized by the state.) You should read the form through very carefully, and if you need help in deciphering the terms, contact the Legal Referral Service of your local bar association. (See appendix for addresses of national, state, and county bar associations.) But do this BEFORE you sign anything. This method may sound a bit extreme in view of the fact that any competent attorney will usually explain the points of a contingent-retainer agreement if you ask him. Many attorneys do not even wait to be asked and will, in fact, explain the terms to you outright.

The bottom line is this: Whether you are dealing with a flat fee, a per-hour arrangement, or a contingency-retainer, never hesitate to ask questions concerning the payment of all monies to an attorney. Only in this way can you avoid misunderstandings. Know what you are paying for and what you are being charged for.

WHAT RESULTS TO EXPECT

You can expect that anything told to your attorney in confidence will remain strictly privileged and will not be revealed to anyone.

You can expect that the attorney will conduct himself in a professional manner and therefore should not be called upon to cheat, lie, or support perjury in any way for the benefit of his client.

You can expect that the attorney will analyze the requests of his client, assemble all the necessary facts, and determine (and apply) the law to the situations involved. This may require extensive research, appearances in court or conferences, and the like. Whatever is required should be done by the attorney within the bounds set forth by the American Bar Association, his own state bar association, and the laws of the jurisdiction in which he practices.

You can expect that your attorney will be responsive to your needs and to your inquiries relative to the progress of your case. This does not mean that you call the attorney seventeen times a day with minuscule or academic problems. Good common sense is mandated in dealing with an attorney as to his time, because you may be charged for it.

Keep in mind that for every case won, a case is lost. This does not mean that the attorney who has lost a case has not handled it properly; it simply means that the law may have been against *you*.

A client often grumbles that when he places his case in the hands of an attorney, he loses control of it. But that's usually his own fault. Lawyers must follow instructions. It is therefore up to you to express clearly any limitations and to define the areas of responsibility. Otherwise, you will have to accept the risk for the lawyer acting on his own. This is why you should have an idea of what you want your lawyer to do. Discuss everything openly so that the lawyer understands what the problem is and what you want him to do about it.

Most lawyers are also expert at helping clients resolve disputes out of court by attempting to find practical, useful solutions. In effect, you are paying for a professional problem-solver.

The results depend on your problem and what you want the lawyer to do. The ABA survey reported that 90 percent of the people interviewed said that the lawyer had completed the work by the end of the first consultation (or at some later time), and that only 10 percent reported the lawyer did not handle the case or the involvement was terminated before the work was completed. Actually, 83 percent of those interviewed gave their lawyers top rating for competence.

In fact, on the results achieved, note these figures representing the extent to which the client obtained what he had sought from the lawyers:

Estate planning	100%	Governmental	69%
Real property	98%	Criminal	58%
Estate settlement	96%	Employment	43%
Marital	90%	Torts	35%
Consumer	75%		

With respect to fees, 93 percent thought that they were charged no more than other lawyers would have charged for the same service.

How were lawyers rated on honesty? Actually, they were rated the highest on that aspect—and lowest on keeping their clients apprised of what was happening with their case. Promptness, explaining matters fully, and paying attention to the client were rated well below honesty but higher than interest and concern about the client's problems.

Did people who used lawyers represent a special group of troublemakers? Although 90 percent said no, 44 percent felt that a person should first exhaust other alternatives before consulting a lawyer. Interestingly enough, 83 percent felt that many people do not go to lawyers because they have no way of knowing which lawyer is competent to handle their particular problem; and 84 percent felt let down because of the lack of progress reports from the lawyer to the client.

TO SUMMARIZE

So, what should you keep in mind? Two things: First, discuss fees openly and in detail to understand what time is involved for your particular problem. And second, know what type of lawyer is good for you, and in what situations. This book has tried to answer that for you. The public thinks that simply because attorneys have gone to law school they have the answers to every legal question. That is a mistake. Don't be burned by it.

In Conclusion

We have looked at those instances when you should consult a lawyer. It is readily acknowledged that there is a difference between when you *should* and when you *must* obtain legal services. However, the line between these situations is not always that clear. Remember, that in criminal cases of any serious nature, you must have a lawyer. It would be sheer folly to try to represent yourself when charged with the commission of a felony or other serious offense. The gravity of the penalties if you are found guilty, the fact that you may be held in jail for weeks without a hearing because criminal courts are so congested, the risk that bail may be set at a figure you cannot afford to pay, and the intricacies of criminal procedure in general—all argue the wisdom of consulting a lawyer at once.

When don't you really need a lawyer? If you require money for an emergency, see your local banker. If you have tax problems, see your accountant. If you are buying a house in a "routine" situation (watch this carefully) from a well-known builder with a fine reputation, you can usually rely on a real-estate agent, on the title company that insures your title to the property, or on the attorney for the bank or some other institution that will hold the mortgage.

If you are not receiving social security or unemployment compensation checks to which you are entitled, government officials must help you.

Also, you may not need a lawyer for a claim involving a small amount of money. Remember small claims court.

Of course, the spiral turns the other way too. There is scarcely an area of American life in which social, political, and economic developments are not increasing the demand for lawyers. Disputes are proliferating, particularly the high-volume types: automobile-accident claims, family squabbles, labor grievances, business altercations, claims against massive corporations, and complaints against the government.

A lot of people, though, do try to handle many things themselves. Modern pretrial procedures are so expensive and time-consuming (substantially increasing the cost to the parties) that they create a motivation among laypersons to return to less predictable methods for resolving disputes. It is vitally important, then, to recognize whether or not a lawyer is required. You don't want to get caught in the man-who-tries-to-be-his-own-lawyer-has-a-fool-for-a-client trap, but you also don't want to leap too quickly when you have no reason.

Remember, what you decide can easily determine the amount of money that you may win, but probably more importantly, what you may *lose*.

Appendix

The information contained in this Appendix was in effect as of the date this book was written. Addresses and telephone numbers may have changed, and certain requirements and regulations may have been altered.

Note that in many states you can purchase blank legal forms in stationery stores. For example, in New York, there are the Blumberg law blanks. These are available to the general public as a guideline only. The Blumberg catalog specifically calls attention to the fact that the forms should be prepared and executed under the supervision of an attorney to determine their legal sufficiency for the use intended, with or without change. Among the forms available are *Notice of Intention to Make Claim* (for accident cases), *Bargain and Sale Deed*, *Apartment Lease, Application for a Patent,* and a form for verification of an automobile repair bill. If you want to see what a certain form looks like, you can, but the authors caution you about using any of these forms without proper legal guidance.

Chapter 1:   Consumer Protection

CONSUMER PROTECTION ORGANIZATIONS

Listed below by subject are the major government agencies and private organizations concerned with consumer rights or environmental matters.

Air Travel

Complaints should be directed to: Office of Consumer Affairs, Civil Aeronautics Board, 1825 Connecticut Avenue, N.W., Washington, DC 20428. A hotline number is open twenty-four hours a day, seven days a week: (202) 382-7735. In addition, you can contact the Aviation Consumer Action Panel, 1346 Connecticut Avenue, N.W., Washington, DC 20036.

Appliances

Most companies have toll-free lines. For example, if you have a complaint against Whirlpool, call (800) 253-1301; for Westinghouse, (800) 245-0600; for Admiral, (800) 447-1350.

This industry has also set up a mediation panel to help resolve consumer complaints: Major Appliance Consumer Action Panel, 20 North Wacker Drive, Chicago, IL 60606; telephone (312) 236-3165.

Automobiles

If you can't get satisfaction from your neighborhood dealer, contact the manufacturer:

American Motors Corporation

14250 Plymouth Road
Detroit, MI 48232

Chrysler Corporation

P.O. Box 1086
Detroit, MI 48221

Ford Motor Company

c/o Ford Customer Service Division
Box 1514
19855 West Outer Drive
Dearborn, MI 48121

General Motors Corporation

Buick Motor Division
902 East Hamilton Avenue
Flint, MI 48550

Cadillac Motor Car Division
  2860 Clark Avenue
  Detroit, MI 48232
Chevrolet Motor Division
  GM Building,
  Detroit, MI 48202
Oldsmobile Division
  920 Townsend Street
  Lansing, MI 48921
Pontiac Motor Division
  1 Pontiac Plaza
  Pontiac, MI 48053

If you are concerned with automobile safety, send all complaints to the National Transportation Safety Board, U.S. Department of Transportation, Washington, DC 20591. You can also contact the Office of Defects Investigation at the Department of Transportation and the Center for Auto Safety, Box 7250, Ben Franklin Station, Washington, DC 20044.

If you have a problem concerning automobile insurance, write to the Insurance Information Institute, which has three addresses:

110 William Street, New York, NY 10038

1266 National Press Building, 529 Fourteenth Street, N.W., Washington, DC 20004

400 Montgomery Street, San Francisco, CA 94104

Communications

All complaints relating to radio or television broadcasting should be directed to the Federal Communications Commission, 1919 M Street, N.W., Washington, DC 20554.

Counseling Services

If you need help with psychiatric problems or in any number of family-related areas, contact a local voluntary family-service agency in your area or write to any of the following organizations for information:

Family Service Association of America
44 East Twenty-third Street
New York, NY 10010

Community Services Administration
Department of Health, Education and Welfare
330 C Street, S.W.
Washington, DC 20201

YMCA
291 Broadway
New York, NY 10007

YWCA
600 Lexington Avenue
New York, NY 10022

Credit

If you feel you are a victim of unfair business practices, call or write your nearest office of the Federal Trade Commission. The FTC watches over deceptive advertising, illegal business tactics, consumer frauds, violations of truth in lending, and other kinds of unfair trade practices. The main office is Bureau of Consumer Protection, Federal Trade Commission, Washington, DC 20580. The regional offices are:

CALIFORNIA

450 Golden Gate Avenue
Box 36005
San Francisco 94102

Federal Building
11000 Wilshire Boulevard
Los Angeles 90024

GEORGIA

730 Peachtree Street
Atlanta 30308

ILLINOIS

55 East Monroe Street
Chicago 60603

MASSACHUSETTS

John F. Kennedy Federal Building
Government Center
Boston 02203

MISSOURI

Federal Office Building
911 Walnut Street
Kansas City 64106

NEW YORK

Federal Building
26 Federal Plaza
New York 10007

OHIO

Federal Office Building
1240 East Ninth St.
Cleveland 44199

WASHINGTON

1511 Third Avenue
Seattle 98101

If the problem involves a bank, contact either the bank itself or the following:

1. If it's a state-chartered bank that is a member of the Federal Reserve System, write to the Truth-in-Lending Officer in care of the Federal Reserve Bank in any of the following locations:

CALIFORNIA

400 Sansome Street
San Francisco 94120

GEORGIA

104 Marietta Street, N.W.
Atlanta 30303

ILLINOIS

230 South LaSalle Street
Chicago 60690

MASSACHUSETTS

30 Pearl Street
Boston 02106

MINNESOTA

250 Marquette Avenue
Minneapolis 55480

MISSOURI

925 Grand Avenue
Kansas City 64198

MISSOURI—cont.

411 Locust Street
St. Louis 63166

NEW YORK

33 Liberty Street
New York 10045

OHIO

1455 East Sixth Street
Cleveland 44101

PENNSYLVANIA

925 Chestnut Street
Philadelphia 19101

TEXAS

400 South Akard Street
Dallas 75222

VIRGINIA

100 North Ninth Street
Richmond 23261

2. If the bank is not a member of the Federal Reserve System, write to the Division of Examination, Federal Deposit Insurance Corporation, 550 Seventeenth Street, N.W., Washington, DC 20429

3. If it's a national bank, contact the Comptroller of the Currency, United States Department of the Treasury, Washington, DC 20220.

If you're dealing with a credit union, and it's a federally chartered one, write to the National Credit Union Administration, Office of Examination, 2025 M Street, N.W., Washington, DC 20456. If it's a state-chartered union, contact the Department of Banking in your state or the particular state agency dealing with credit unions.

If you are rated as a bad credit risk and you believe the information to be inaccurate, contact the Associated Credit Bureaus, Inc., 6767 Southwest Freeway, Houston, TX 77036. You can also get in touch with the local office of the Federal Trade Commission, which enforces the Fair Credit Reporting Act.

Environmental

The various organizations concerned with environmental protection and what they do are:

The Environmental Defense Fund, 162 Old Town Road, East Setauket, NY 11733; concerned with preserving a healthful environment through court action.

The Center for Science in the Public Interest, 1779 Church Street, N.W., Washington, DC 20036; helps find technical expertise to press the matter in court.

Consumer Alliance, Inc., P.O. Box 11773, Palo Alto, CA 94306; offers ways in which you can help minimize adverse effects on the environment.

The following groups publish bulletins and newsletters on a regular basis and lobby, educate, and bring legal action to protect the environment:

Environmental Action, Inc., 1346 Connecticut Avenue, N.W., Washington, DC 20036

National Audubon Society, 950 Third Avenue, New York, NY 10022

Sierra Club, 1050 Mills Tower, San Francisco, CA 94104

Wilderness Society, 1901 Pennsylvania Avenue, N.W., Washington, DC 20006

Food and Drugs

All complaints should be reported to the nearest office of the Food and Drug Administration (FDA). The national headquarters are located at 5600 Fishers Lane, Rockville, MD 20852.

The district offices are:

CALIFORNIA

John L. Harvey Bldg.
1521 West Pico Blvd.
Los Angeles 90015

CALIFORNIA—cont.

Room 518
50 Fulton Street
San Francisco 94102

COLORADO

513 New Customhouse
Denver 80202

GEORGIA

60 Eighth Street, N.E.
Atlanta 30309

ILLINOIS

Room 1222, Main Post Office
Chicago 60607

LOUISIANA

423 Canal Street
New Orleans 70130

MASSACHUSETTS

585 Commercial Street
Boston 02109

MICHIGAN

1560 East Jefferson Avenue
Detroit 48207

MINNESOTA

240 Hennepin Avenue
Minneapolis 55401

MISSOURI

1009 Cherry Street
Kansas City 64106

NEW JERSEY

Room 831
970 Broad Street
Newark 07102

NEW YORK

Room 700
850 Third Avenue
Brooklyn 11232

599 Delaware Avenue
Buffalo 14202

OHIO

Paul B. Dunbar Bldg.
1141 Central Parkway
Cincinnati 45202

PENNSYLVANIA

Room 1204
U.S. Custom House Bldg.
2nd and Chestnut Streets
Philadelphia 19106

PUERTO RICO

P.O. Box 4427
Old San Juan Station
San Juan 00905

TEXAS

3032 Bryan Street
Dallas 75204

WASHINGTON

Room 5003
Federal Office Bldg.
901 First Avenue
Seattle 98104

If you feel your supermarket or grocer's scales are inaccurate, contact your state Bureau of Weights and Measures, or write to the Office of Weights and Measures, National Bureau of Standards, Washington, DC 20234.

Furniture

Direct all complaints to the furniture dealer and the manufacturer. If you receive no satisfaction, contact the Furniture Industry Consumer Advisory Panel, P.O. Box 951, High Point, NC 27261. The hotline number is (919) 885-5065.

Health

The various national organizations are:

American Medical Association
535 North Dearborn Street
Chicago, IL 60610

American Dental Association
211 East Chicago Avenue
Chicago, IL 60611

American Psychiatric Association
1700 Eighteenth Street, N.W.
Washington, DC 20009

American Public Health Association
1015 Eighteenth Street, N.W.
Washington, DC 20036

National Medical Association
2109 E Street, N.W.
Washington, DC 20006

United States Public Health Service
5600 Fishers Lane
Rockville, MD 20852

Most serious complaints about medical service should be directed to your state's office of Consumer Health Affairs and to your local health or county medical societies. If there is a problem with a hospital, contact the American Hospital Association, 840 North Lake Shore Drive, Chicago, IL 60611

If you would like information on health care, a number of pamphlets are offered by the government. Write to the Superintendent of Documents, U.S. Government Printing Office, Washington, DC 20402, for a list of all government publications. The prices are nominal; many are even free.

Insurance

Direct questions to the State Insurance Department in your state capital or write to the Institute of Life Insurance and Health Insurance, 277 Park Avenue, New York, NY 10017

In the field of health insurance, a number of superb booklets are published by the Pennsylvania Insurance Department. Write to that department in Harrisburg or to Consumer News, Inc. 813 National Press Building, Washington, DC 20045.

Complaints can be directed to the Insurance Consumer Action Panel, in care of National Association of Mutual Insurance Agents, 1511 K Street, N.W., Washington, DC 20005.

Mail-Order Sales

Complaints about mail fraud should be directed to the Office of the Chief Postal Inspector, U.S. Postal Service, Washington, DC 20260. You can also contact the Consumer Service Director, Direct Mail Marketing Association, 230 Park Avenue, New York, NY 10017.

If your complaint is with a door-to-door salesman, contact the Direct Selling Association, 1730 M Street, N.W., Washington, DC 20036.

Mortgages

Questions involving a home mortgage should be directed to the nearest office of the Veterans Administration (if it's a VA mortgage) or the Federal Housing Administration (FHA). The national headquarters of the FHA is in care of the Department of Housing and Urban Development, 451 Seventh Street, S.W., Washington, DC 20410. VA headquarters are located at 810 Vermont Avenue, Washington, DC 20420.

Moving

All moves from state to state come under the protection of the Interstate Commerce Commission. Complaints should be directed to that commission to the attention Bureau of Operations, Washington, DC 20423. The hotline number is (202) 343-4761. Moves within the same state are covered by the law of the particular jurisdiction, so all complaints should be made to the Department of Transportation in your state.

Post Office

Direct all problems to your local postmaster. If you don't get results, contact the Consumer Advocate, United States Postal Service, 475 L'enfant Plaza West, S.W., Washington, DC 20260.

Product Safety

Complaints about unsafe products should be made to the Consumer Product Safety Commission, Washington, DC 20207. Regional offices are:

CALIFORNIA

Suite 1100
3600 Wilshire Boulevard
Los Angeles 90010

Room 558
50 Fulton Street
San Francisco 94102

COLORADO

Suite 938
Guaranty Bank Building
817 Seventeenth Street
Denver 80202

GEORGIA

1330 West Peachtree Street, N.W.
Atlanta 30309

ILLINOIS

1 North Wacker Drive
Chicago 60606

LOUISIANA

International Trade Mart, Suite
  414
2 Canal Street
New Orleans 70013

MASSACHUSETTS

408 Atlantic Avenue

MINNESOTA

Room 650
Federal Building, Fort Snelling
Twin Cities 55111

MISSOURI

Room 1905
911 Walnut Street
Kansas City 64106

NEW YORK

830 Third Avenue
Brooklyn 11232

OHIO

DEB Annex 21046
Brookpark Road
Cleveland 44135

PENNSYLVANIA

Continental Building
400 Market Street
Philadelphia 19106

TEXAS

500 South Ervay
Dallas 75201

WASHINGTON

1131 Federal Building
909 First Avenue

The Product Safety Commission can also be contacted through a hotline number: (800) 638-2666. If you're not quite sure to whom you should be complaining, the U.S. General Services Administration has set up Federal Information centers in thirty-seven cities. Contact any of these centers to find out where you can obtain the answer to your problem.

ARIZONA

Federal Building
230 North First Avenue
Phoenix 85020
(602) 261-3313

CALIFORNIA

Federal Building
300 North Los Angeles Street
Los Angeles 90012
(213) 688-3800

Federal Building
650 Capitol Mall
Sacramento 95814
(916) 440-3344

202 C Street
San Diego 92101
(714) 293-6030

Federal Building
450 Golden Gate Avenue
San Francisco 94102
(415) 556-6600

COLORADO

Federal Building
1961 Stout Street
Denver 80202
(303) 837-3602

DISTRICT OF COLUMBIA

Seventh and D Streets, N.W.
Washington 20407
(202) 755-8660

FLORIDA

Federal Building
51 S.W. First Avenue
Miami 33130
(305) 350-4155

Federal Building
144 First Avenue S
St. Petersburg 33701
(813) 893-3495

GEORGIA

Federal Building
275 Peachtree Street, N.E.
Atlanta 30303
(404) 526-6891

HAWAII

U.S. Post Office
335 Merchant Street
Honolulu 96813
(808) 546-8620

ILLINOIS

Everett McKinley Dirksen Building
219 South Dearborn Street
Chicago 60604
(312) 353-4242

INDIANA

Federal Building
575 North Pennsylvania Street
Indianapolis 46204
(317) 269-7373

KENTUCKY

Federal Building
600 Federal Place
Louisville 40202
(502) 582-6261

LOUISIANA

Federal Building
701 Loyola Avenue
New Orleans 70113
(504) 589-6696

MARYLAND

Federal Building
31 Hopkins Plaza
Baltimore 21201
(301) 962-4980

MASSACHUSETTS

John F. Kennedy Federal Building
Government Center
Boston 02203
(617) 223-7121

MICHIGAN

Federal Building
447 Michigan Avenue
Detroit 48226
(313) 226-7016

MINNESOTA

Federal Building
110 South Fourth Street
Minneapolis 55401
(612) 725-2073

MISSOURI

Federal Building
601 East Twelfth Street
Kansas City 64106
(816) 374-2466

MISSOURI—cont.

Federal Building
1520 Market Street
St. Louis 63103
(314) 425-4106

NEBRASKA

Federal Building
215 North Seventeenth Street
Omaha 68102
(402) 221-3353

NEW JERSEY

Federal Building
970 Broad Street
Newark 07102
(201) 645-3600

NEW MEXICO

Federal Building
500 Gold Avenue, S.W.
Albuquerque 87101
(505) 766-3091

NEW YORK

Federal Building
111 West Huron Street
Buffalo 14202
(716) 842-5770

Federal Office Building
26 Federal Plaza
New York 10007
(212) 264-4464

OHIO

Federal Building
550 Main Street
Cincinnati 45202
(513) 684-2801

OHIO—cont.

Federal Building
1240 East Ninth Street
Cleveland 44199
(216) 522-4040

OKLAHOMA

Federal Office Building
201 N.W. Third Street
Oklahoma City 73102
(405) 231-4868

OREGON

Federal Building
1220 S.W. Third Avenue
Portland 97204
(503) 221-2222

PENNSYLVANIA

Federal Building
600 Arch Street
Philadelphia 19106
(215) 597-7042

Federal Building
1000 Liberty Avenue
Pittsburgh 15222
(412) 644-3456

TENNESSEE

Federal Building
167 North Main Street
Memphis 38103
(901) 534-3285

TEXAS

Federal Building
819 Taylor Street
Fort Worth 76102
(817) 334-3624

Federal Building
515 Rusk Avenue
Houston 77002
(713) 226-5711

UTAH

Federal Building
125 South State Street
Salt Lake City 84138
(801) 524-5353

WASHINGTON

Federal Building
915 Second Avenue
Seattle 98174
(206) 442-0570

If you are not near any of the above centers, you can call the following toll-free numbers:

Alabama, 322-8591 (Birmingham)
Arizona, 622-1511 (Tucson)
Arkansas, 378-6177 (Little Rock)
California, 275-7422 (San Jose)
Colorado, 471-9491 (Colorado Springs); 544-9523 (Pueblo)
Connecticut, 527-2617 (Hartford); 624-4720 (New Haven)
Florida, 522-8531 (Ft. Lauderdale); 354-4756 (Jacksonville); 229-7911 (Tampa); 833-7566 (West Palm Beach)
Iowa, 282-9091 (Des Moines)
Kansas, 232-7229 (Topeka); 263-6931 (Wichita)
Missouri, 233-8206 (St. Joseph)

New Jersey, 396-4400 (Trenton)
New Mexico, 983-7743 (Santa Fe)
New York, 463-4421 (Albany); 546-5075 (Rochester); 476-8545 (Syracuse)
North Carolina, 376-3600 (Charlotte)
Ohio, 375-5475 (Akron); 221-1014 (Columbus); 223-7377 (Dayton); 244-8625 (Toledo)
Oklahoma, 548-4193 (Tulsa)
Pennsylvania, 346-7081 (Scranton)
Rhode Island, 331-5565 (Providence)
Tennessee, 265-8231 (Chattanooga); 242-5056 (Nashville)
Texas, 472-5494 (Austin); 749-2131 (Dallas); 224-4471 (San Antonio)
Utah, 399-1347 (Ogden)
Washington, 383-5230 (Tacoma)
Wisconsin, 271-2273 (Milwaukee)

Other organizations that deal with consumer problems and product liability: Common Cause, 2030 M Street, N.W., Washington, DC 20036, the largest citizens lobby group in the country; Consumer Federation of America, 1012 Fourteenth Street, N.W., Washington, DC 20005, a federation of hundreds of state and local consumer groups helping to publicize important issues; Consumers Union, 256 Washington Street, Mount Vernon, NY 10550, publishes *Consumer Reports* magazine and also participates in lawsuits on behalf of consumers; and the Office of Consumer Affairs, Washington, DC 20201; a government agency dealing with all kinds of consumer problems.

Social Security

For problems concerning social security, contact your local office (under "United States Government" in the phone book), or write to the Social Security Administration, 6401 Security Boulevard, Baltimore, MD 21235.

Stocks

Complaints about security transactions should be directed to the nearest regional office of the Securities and Exchange Commission, or to Securities and Exchange Commission, 500 North Capitol Street, N.W., Washington DC 20549.

Taxes

Complaints, questions, and inquiries about taxes should be directed to your local Internal Revenue Service Office. The main office is in Washington, DC 20224. A number of toll-free information numbers can be found in your telephone book under "United States Government." For information on tax-court matters, contact the Clerk of the Court, United States Tax Court, Washington, DC 20217.

Tenant's Rights

Advice on landlord/tenant relations can be obtained from the National Tenants Organization, 425 Thirteenth Street, N.W., Washington, DC 20004

For general information on a number of products, services, and problems in the field of consumer protection, write to Consumer Information, Pueblo, CO 81009, and ask for the "Consumer Information Index" to pamphlets, many of which are free. Another good source is the *Directory of Consumer Protection*, available from Academic Media, 32 Lincoln Avenue, Orange, NJ 07050, or from your local public library. This directory lists various private and governmental agencies throughout the United States.

Chapter 2: Human Rights

Race discrimination: Contact the National Association for the Advancement of Colored People, 1790 Broadway, New York, NY 10019, or the American Civil Liberties Union, 22 East 40th Street, New York, NY 10016. There are usually local branches of these two organizations that can help you.

Sex discrimination: Write to the Women's Bureau of the United States Department of Labor, Washington, DC 20036; the Center for Women's Policy Studies, 2000 P Street, N.W., Washington, DC 20036; and the National Organization for Women, Suite 1615, 5 South Wabash, Chicago, IL 60603.

Discrimination in housing: Contact the Secretary of Housing and Urban Development, Washington, DC 20410.

Discrimination in employment: Contact the Equal Employment Opportunity Commission, Washington, DC 20506, or the one in your area. You can also write to the Wage and Hour Division, Employment Standards Administration, U.S. Department of Labor, Washington, DC 20210 (there are some 350 regional offices).

If you believe the federal government has been discriminatory in its employment practices, complain to the U.S. Civil Service Commission, 1900 E Street, N.W., Washington, DC 20415. At the same time, you can also address your complaint to your state's Fair Employment Commission or Human Rights Agency, and to the United States Commission on Civil Rights, Washington, DC 20425.

Discrimination in lending: The Federal Equal Credit Opportunity Act bars lenders of money from discriminating on the basis of sex or marital status. If your loan has been turned down because of your sex or marital status, contact the Office of Saver and Consumer Affairs, Federal Reserve System, Washington, DC 20551.

Pensions: If you have any complaint about your company's pension plan, contact the Office of Employee Benefit Security in your area. The Department of Labor in Washington has been watching all pension plans under the 1974 Pension Reform Law, its intention being to curb abuses. Complaints can be made to any of the following offices, and they will conduct an investigation:

CALIFORNIA

300 North Los Angeles Street
Los Angeles 90012

100 McAllister Street
San Francisco 94102

COLORADO

1020 Fifteenth Street
Denver 80202

FLORIDA

18350 Northwest Second Avenue
Miami 33169

GEORGIA

1371 Peachtree Street, N.E.
Atlanta 30309

HAWAII

1833 Kalakaua Avenue
Honolulu 96815

ILLINOIS

219 South Dearborn Street
Chicago 60604

LOUISIANA

600 South Street
New Orleans 70130

MASSACHUSETTS

110 Tremont Street
Boston 02108

MICHIGAN

234 State Street
Detroit 48226

MINNESOTA

110 South Fourth Street
Minneapolis 55401

MISSOURI

911 Walnut Street
Kansas City 64106

NEW JERSEY

9 Clinton Street
Newark 07102

NEW YORK

111 West Huron Street
Buffalo 14202

26 Federal Plaza
New York 10007

OHIO

1240 East Ninth Street
Cleveland 44199

PENNSYLVANIA

600 Arch Street
Philadelphia 19106

1000 Liberty Avenue
Pittsburgh 15222

PUERTO RICO

605 Condado Avenue
Santurce 00907

TENNESSEE

1808 West End Building
Nashville 37203

TEXAS

Bryan and Ervay Streets
Dallas 75221

WASHINGTON

506 Second Avenue
Seattle 98104

You can also send your complaint to the Office of Employee Benefit Security, Washington, D.C. 20044.

For additional information concerning pension plans and your rights, contact the Association of Private Pension and Welfare Plans, Inc., 1028 Connecticut Avenue, N.W., Washington, DC 20036, and the American Pension Conference, 358 Fifth Avenue, New York, NY 10001.

Retirement: The primary organizations concerned with the needs of senior citizens:

National Council of Senior Citizens
1511 K Street, N.W.
Washington, DC 20005

American Association of Retired Persons
1909 K Street, N.W.
Washington, DC 20006

National Council on the Aging
200 Park Avenue South
New York, NY 10010

Department of Health, Education and Welfare
Washington, DC 20201

Most states also have special commissions on aging and the elderly.

Right to Privacy: Under the Privacy Act of 1974, you can obtain all information maintained by the federal government relating to you simply by writing the appropriate governmental agency.

* For information relating to food products, write to the Director for Information, Office of Investigation, Department of Agriculture, Washington, DC 20250

* For business matters, write to the Director, Office of Organization and Management, U.S. Department of Commerce, Washington, DC 20230

* For military records, write to the Department of Defense Privacy Board, Washington, DC 20301

* For health, education, and welfare, write to the Director, Office of Investigations and Security, Room 4524, North Building, U.S. Department of Health, Education and Welfare, 330 Independence Avenue, S.W., Washington, DC 20201

* For property matters, write to the Chief, Division of General Services, Office of Management Operations, Department of the Interior, Eighteenth and C Streets, N.W., Washington, DC 20240

* For legal matters, including prison records, write to the Assistant Attorney General, U.S. Department of Justice, Washington, DC 20530

* For foreign matters, write to the Director, Foreign Affairs Document and Reference Center, Room 1239, Department of State, 2201 C Street, N.W., Washington, DC 20520

* For transportation matters, write to the Privacy Act Coordinator, Executive Secretariat, Room 5217, Department of Transportation Headquarters Building, Washington, DC 20590

* For money matters, write to the Administrative Officer, Department of the Treasury, Washington, DC 20220

* For information about any CIA system of records you believe may contain information about you, write to the Privacy Act Coordinator, Central Intelligence Agency, Washington, DC 20505

* For information relating to civil rights, write to the General Counsel, Office of General Counsel, Room 600, U.S. Commission on Civil Rights, 1121 Vermont Avenue, N.W., Washington, DC 20425

* For information relating to broadcasting operations, write to the Chief, Broadcast Bureau, 1919 M Street, N.W., Washington, DC 20554

* For information relating to unions, write to the Executive Assistant, National Labor Relations Board, 1717 Pennsylvania Avenue, N.W., Washington, DC 20570

* For information about any National Security Council system of records you believe contains information about you, write to the Staff Secretary, National Security Council, Old Executive Office Building, Washington, DC 20506

* For information about any Securities and Exchange Commission system of records you believe contains records about you, write to the Securities and Exchange Commission, Public Reference Section, 1100 L Street, N.W., Washington, DC 20249

* For information about any Small Business Administration system of records, write to the Central Office of the Small Business Administration, 1441 L Street, N.W., Washington, DC 20416

* For information about any United States Information Agency records, write to the Assistant Director (USIA), Public Information, 1750 Pennsylvania Avenue, N.W., Washington, DC 20547

* For veterans, information can be obtained by writing to the Assistant General Counsel (024), Veterans Administration Central Office, Washington, DC 20420

Federal Register: For a complete digest of all addresses relating to governmental agencies, you can obtain the *Federal Register: Protecting Your Right to Privacy*, a digest of systems of records, agency rules, and research aids published by the Office of the Federal Register, National Archives and Records Service, General Services Administration. It can be purchased by writing to The National Archives of the United States, Washington, D.C.

Sample Name-Change Petition - New York State

SUPREME COURT OF THE STATE OF NEW YORK
COUNTY OF

———————————————————————————— x

Application of   Petition
for leave to change his/her name to   Index No.

———————————————————————————— x

   1. My name is
   2. I was born on   19   , at   ,

and am presently   years of age. Annexed hereto is my birth certificate (or a
certified transcript of my birth certificate or a certificate of the Commissioner of
Health of   , that my birth certificate is not available).
   3. My present residence is
   4. The name I propose to assume is
   5. I have never been convicted of a crime (or I have been convicted of the
following crimes:).
   6. I have never been adjudicated a bankrupt.
   7. I am a citizen of the United States and have been such for at least six
months prior to making this application.
   8. I am married (or I am single and have never been married).
   9. There are no judgments or liens of record against me or against any
property in my name and there is no action or proceeding pending to which I am a
party (or state details of judgments, liens, actions or proceedings).
   10. The grounds of this application are as follows: (set forth reasons why change
of name is sought).
   11. The change of name I request is not intended to deceive or mislead.
   12. No previous application has been made for this relief.

   WHEREFORE, petitioner requests that an order be granted permitting
him/her to assume the name

Dated:

———————————————————————
                       Petitioner

Address:

(Verification)

Chapter 3:   Family Matters

Divorce: All the states have adultery as a ground for divorce. Most will also recognize habitual use of drugs and felony convictions as grounds. In fact, even in those states where there is no-fault, certain grounds for divorce are still on the books.

Various quirks exist in the laws of some states, so it is important to check the specific law in your jurisdiction. For example, Oklahoma has a six-month residency but requires that thirty days must be spent in the county in which the divorce is sought. In California, residency within a particular county is three months. There are just too many variables, so this table should be used merely as a guide.

STATE REQUIREMENTS AND GROUNDS FOR DIVORCE

ALABAMA: Residency in state, 6 months; applicable no-fault law, yes; grounds for divorce, adultery, cruelty, insanity, life imprisonment, physical defects.

ALASKA: Residency in state: 1 year; applicable no-fault law, no; grounds for divorce, adultery, cruelty, incompatibility, insanity, life imprisonment.

ARIZONA: Residency in state, 3 months; applicable no-fault law, yes; grounds for divorce, irreconcilable or irretrievable differences.

ARKANSAS: Residency in state, 2 months; applicable no-fault law, no; grounds for divorce, adultery, bigamy, cruelty, insanity, life imprisonment, separation.

CALIFORNIA: Residency in state, 6 months; applicable no-fault law, yes; grounds for divorce, irreconcilable or irretrievable differences; also, postmarital insanity.

COLORADO: Residency in state, 3 months; applicable no-fault law, yes; grounds for divorce, irreconcilable or irretrievable differences.

CONNECTICUT: Residency in state, 1 year; applicable no-fault law, no; grounds for divorce, adultery, cruelty, fraud, insanity, life imprisonment, separation.

DELAWARE: Residency in state, 1 year; applicable no-fault law, yes; grounds for divorce, adultery, bigamy, cruelty, fraud, incompatibility, life imprisonment, separation.

DISTRICT OF COLUMBIA: Residency in state, 1 year; applicable no-fault law, no; grounds for divorce, adultery, separation.

FLORIDA: Residency in state, 6 months; applicable no-fault law, yes; grounds for divorce, irreconcilable or irretrievable differences.

GEORGIA: Residency in state, 6 months; applicable no-fault law, yes; grounds for divorce, adultery, cruelty, fraud, insanity, sexual incapacity.

HAWAII: Residency in state, 1 year; applicable no-fault law, yes; grounds for divorce, irreconcilable or irretrievable differences.

IDAHO: Residency in state, 6 weeks; applicable no-fault law, yes; grounds for divorce, adultery, cruelty, insanity, separation, gross neglect.

ILLINOIS: Residency in state, 1 year; applicable no-fault law, no; grounds for divorce, adultery, attempted murder of spouse, bigamy, cruelty, fraud, venereal disease, sexual incapacity.

INDIANA: Residency in state, 1 year; applicable no-fault law, no; grounds for divorce, adultery, cruelty, insanity, sexual incapacity.

IOWA: Residency in state, 1 year; applicable no-fault law, yes; grounds for divorce, irreconcilable or irretrievable differences.

KANSAS: Residency in state, 6 months; applicable no-fault law, no; grounds for divorce, adultery, cruelty, incompatibility, life imprisonment, gross neglect.

KENTUCKY: Residency in state, 6 months; applicable no-fault law, yes; grounds for divorce, irreconcilable differences.

LOUISIANA: Residency in state, 2 years; applicable no-fault law, no; grounds for divorce, adultery, attempted murder of spouse, cruelty, separation.

MAINE: Residency in state, 6 months; applicable no-fault law, no; grounds for divorce, adultery, cruelty, life imprisonment, sexual incapacity.

MARYLAND: Residency in state, 1 year; applicable no-fault law, no; grounds for divorce, adultery, bigamy, insanity, separation, sexual incapacity.

MASSACHUSETTS: Residency in state, 2 years; applicable no-fault law, no; grounds for divorce, adultery, cruelty, separation, life imprisonment, sexual incapacity.

MICHIGAN: Residency in state, 1 year; applicable no-fault law, yes; grounds for divorce, irreconcilable or irretrievable differences.

MINNESOTA: Residency in state, 1 year; applicable no-fault law, yes; grounds for divorce, adultery, separation, sexual incapacity.

MISSISSIPPI: Residency in state, 1 year; applicable no-fault law, no; grounds for divorce, adultery, bigamy, cruelty, insanity, life imprisonment, sexual incapacity.

MISSOURI: Residency in state, 1 year; applicable no-fault law, no; grounds for divorce, adultery, bigamy, cruelty, personal indignities, sexual incapacity.

MONTANA: Residency in state, 1 year; applicable no-fault law, no; grounds for divorce, adultery, cruelty, insanity, gross neglect.

NEBRASKA: Residency in state, 1 year; applicable no-fault law, yes; grounds for divorce, irreconcilable or irretrievable differences.

NEVADA: Residency in state, 6 weeks; applicable no-fault law, yes; grounds for divorce, irreconcilable or irretrievable differences, and postmarital insanity.

NEW HAMPSHIRE: Residency in state, 1 year; applicable no-fault law, yes; grounds for divorce, adultery, cruelty, separation, sexual incapacity.

NEW JERSEY: Residency in state, 1 year; applicable no-fault law, no; grounds for divorce, adultery, cruelty, insanity, separation, personal indignities.

NEW MEXICO: Residency in state, 1 year; applicable no-fault law, yes; grounds for divorce, adultery, cruelty, incompatibility, insanity, sexual incapacity.

NEW YORK: Residency in state, 2 years; applicable no-fault law, no; grounds for divorce, adultery, cruelty, separation, felony conviction.

NORTH CAROLINA: Residency in state, 6 months; applicable no-fault law, no; grounds for divorce, adultery, insanity, separation, sexual incapacity, physical defect.

NORTH DAKOTA: Residency in state, 1 year; applicable no-fault law, yes; grounds for divorce, adultery, cruelty, insanity, gross neglect.

OHIO: Residency in state, 1 year; applicable no-fault law, no; grounds for divorce, adultery, bigamy, cruelty, fraud, separation, gross neglect, sexual incapacity, insanity.

OKLAHOMA: Residency in state, 6 months; applicable no-fault law, no; grounds for divorce, adultery, cruelty, fraud, incompatibility, insanity, sexual incapacity.

OREGON: Residency in state, 6 months; applicable no-fault law, yes; grounds for divorce, irreconcilable or irretrievable differences.

PENNSYLVANIA: Residency in state, 1 year; applicable no-fault law, no; grounds for divorce, adultery, bigamy, cruelty, duress, fraud, personal indignities, sexual incapacity, physical defect.

RHODE ISLAND: Residency in state, 2 years; applicable no-fault law, no; grounds for divorce, adultery, bigamy, cruelty, separation, life imprisonment, sexual incapacity.

SOUTH CAROLINA: Residency in state, 1 year; applicable no-fault law, no; grounds for divorce, adultery, cruelty, separation.

SOUTH DAKOTA: Residency in state, 1 year; applicable no-fault law, no; grounds for divorce, adultery, cruelty, insanity, gross neglect.

TENNESSEE: Residency in state, 1 year; applicable no-fault law, no; grounds for divorce, adultery, attempted murder of spouse, bigamy, cruelty, separation, personal indignities, sexual incapacity.

TEXAS: Residency in state, 1 year; applicable no-fault law, yes; grounds for divorce, adultery, cruelty, incompatibility, insanity, separation.

UTAH: Residency in state, 3 months; applicable no-fault law, no; grounds for divorce, adultery, cruelty, insanity, separation, gross neglect, sexual incapacity.

VERMONT: Residency in state, 6 months; applicable no-fault law, yes; grounds for divorce, adultery, cruelty, insanity, separation.

VIRGINIA: Residency in state, 1 year; applicable no-fault law, no; grounds for divorce, adultery, separation, life imprisonment, sexual incapacity.

WASHINGTON: Residency in state, 6 months; applicable no-fault law, yes; grounds for divorce, adultery.

WEST VIRGINIA: Residency in state, 1 year; applicable no-fault law, no; grounds for divorce, adultery, cruelty, insanity, separation.

WISCONSIN: Residency in state, 6 months; applicable no-fault law, no; grounds for divorce, adultery, cruelty, separation.

WYOMING: Residency in state, 60 days; applicable no-fault law, no; grounds for divorce, adultery, cruelty, insanity, separation, personal indignities, sexual incapacity, physical defect.

Chapter 5: Business Relationships

The following are the district offices of the Small Business Association. Check with these district offices for local offices in your area.

ALABAMA

908 South Twentieth Street
Birmingham 35205

ALASKA

Suite 200
Anchorage Local Center
1016 West Sixth Street
Anchorage 99501

501 Second Avenue
Fairbanks 99701

ARIZONA

112 North Central Avenue
Phoenix 85004

ARKANSAS

611 Gaines Street
Suite 900
Little Rock 72201

CALIFORNIA

Federal Office Building
1130 O Street
Fresno 93721

CALIFORNIA—cont.

849 South Broadway
Los Angeles 90014

110 West C Street
Suite 705
San Diego 92101

450 Golden Gate Avenue
San Francisco 94102

COLORADO

721 Nineteenth Street
Denver 80202

CONNECTICUT

450 Main Street
Hartford 06103

DELAWARE

Federal Building, Room 3015
844 King Street
Wilmington 19801

DISTRICT OF COLUMBIA

1441 L Street, N.W.
Washington 20416

DISTRICT OF COLUMBIA—cont.

1030 Fifteenth Street, N.W.
Washington 20416

FLORIDA

2222 Ponce De Leon Boulevard
Coral Gables 33134

400 West Bay Street
Jacksonville 32202

GEORGIA

1401 Peachtree Street, N.E.
Atlanta 30309

1030 Peachtree Street, N.E.
Atlanta 30309

HAWAII

1149 Bethel Street
Room 402
Honolulu 96813

IDAHO

216 North Eighth Street
Boise 83701

ILLINOIS

219 South Dearborn Street
Chicago 60655

Ridgley Building, Room 816
502 East Monroe Street
Springfield 62701

INDIANA

Federal Building, Fifth Floor
575 North Pennsylvania Street
Indianapolis 46204

IOWA

210 Walnut Street
Des Moines 50309

KANSAS

120 South Market Street
Wichita 67202

KENTUCKY

Federal Office Building
Room 188
600 Federal Place
Louisville 40202

LOUISIANA

Plaza Tower, Seventeenth Floor
1001 Howard Avenue
New Orleans 70113

MAINE

40 Western Avenue
Augusta 04330

MARYLAND

7800 York Road
Towson 21204

MASSACHUSETTS

150 Causeqay Street
Boston 02114

MICHIGAN

129 Washington Boulevard
Detroit 48226

Bullock Building
201 McClellan Street
Marquette 49885

MINNESOTA

Plymouth Building
12 South Sixth Street
Minneapolis 55402

MISSISSIPPI

Gulf National Life Insurance Building
111 Fred Hais Boulevard
Biloxi 39530

Petroleum Building
Room 690
200 East Pascagoula
Jackson 39201

MISSOURI

911 Walnut Street
Twenty-third Floor
Kansas City 64106

210 North Twelfth Street
St. Louis 63101

MONTANA

613 Helena Avenue
Helena 59601

NEBRASKA

215 North Seventeenth Street
Omaha 68102

NEVADA

301 East Stewart
Las Vegas 89121

NEW HAMPSHIRE

55 Pleasant Street
Concord 03301

NEW JERSEY

970 Broad Street
Room 1635
Newark 07102

NEW MEXICO

Patio Plaza Building
5000 Marble Avenue, N.E.
Albuquerque 87110

NEW YORK

Federal Building, Room 1112
111 West Huron Street
Buffalo 14202

1051 South Main Street
Elmira 14904

26 Federal Plaza
New York City 10009

Fayette and Salina Streets
Syracuse 13202

NORTH CAROLINA

222 South Church Street
Charlotte 28202

NORTH DAKOTA

Federal Office Building
Room 218
653 Second Avenue North
Fargo 58102

OHIO

Federal Building, Room 5524
550 Main Street
Cincinnati 45202

AJC Federal Building
Room 317
1240 East Ninth Street
Cleveland 44199

34 North High Street
Columbus 43215

OKLAHOMA

50 Penn Place
Oklahoma City 73118

OREGON

700 Pittock Block
921 Southwest Washington Street
Portland 97205

PENNSYLVANIA

One Bala Cynwyd Plaza
231 St. Asaphs Road
Bala Cynwyd 19004

1500 North Second Street
Harrisburg 17108

1000 Liberty Avenue
Pittsburgh 15222

Provincial Tower Building
34 South Main Street
Wilkes-Barre 18701

PUERTO RICO

Pan Am Building
255 Ponce De Leon Avenue
Hato Rey 00919

RHODE ISLAND

57 Eddy Street
Providence 02903

SOUTH CAROLINA

1801 Assembly Street
Columbia 29201

SOUTH DAKOTA

Federal Building
515 Ninth Street
Rapid City 57701

Eighth and Main Avenues
Sioux Falls 57102

TENNESSEE

Fidelity Bankers Building
Room 307
502 South Gay Street
Knoxville 37902

Parkway Towers
Room 1012
404 James Robertson Parkway
Nashville 37319

TEXAS

3105 Leopard Street
Corpus Christi 78408

1720 Regal Row, Suite 230
Dallas 75235

1100 Commerce Street
Dallas 75202

417 First National Building
109 North Oregon Street
El Paso 79901

219 East Jackson Street
Harlingen 78580

Niels Esperson Building
808 Travis Street
Houston 77002

712 Federal Office Building
1205 Texas Avenue
Lubbock 79401

505 East Travis Street
Marshall 75670

301 Broadway
San Antonio 78205

UTAH

125 South State Street
Salt Lake City 84138

VERMONT

87 State Street
Montpelier 05602

VIRGINIA

Federal Building, Room 3025
400 North Eighth Street
Richmond 23240

WASHINGTON

Dexter Horton Building
710 Second Avenue
Seattle 98204

WASHINGTON—cont.

651 United States Courthouse
Spokane 99120

WEST VIRGINIA

Charleston National Plaza
Suite 628
Charleston 25301

109 North Third Street
Clarksburg 26301

WISCONSIN

122 West Washington Avenue
Madison 53703

Continental Plaza
735 West Wisconsin Avenue
Milwaukee 53233

WYOMING

Federal Building, Room 4001
100 East B Street
Casper 82601

Chapter 8:   Requirements for a Valid Will

1. Holographic Wills: Certain states recognize the handwritten, or holographic, will *without* the required number of witnesses. Certain states do not.

Recognized

Alaska
Arizona
Arkansas
California
Idaho
Kentucky
Louisiana
Mississippi
Montana
Nevada
North Carolina

North Dakota
Oklahoma
Pennsylvania
South Dakota
Tennessee
Texas
Utah
Virginia
West Virginia
Wyoming

Not Recognized

Alabama
Colorado
Connecticut
Delaware
District of Columbia
Florida
Georgia
Hawaii
Illinois
Indiana
Iowa

Kansas
Maine
Maryland
Massachusetts
Michigan
Minnesota
Missouri
Nebraska
New Hampshire
New Jersey
New Mexico

Not Recognized, continued

New York   South Carolina
Ohio   Vermont
Oregon   Washington
Rhode Island   Wisconsin

2. Minimum Age: Each state has its own requirements as to the minimum age of a party who may draw a will disposing of real and personal property.

State	To Dispose of Real Property	To Dispose of Personal Property
Alabama	21	18
Alaska	19	19
Arizona	18	18
Arkansas	18	18
California	18	18
Colorado	18	18
Connecticut	18	18
Delaware	18	18
District of Columbia	21(M) 18(F)	21(M) 18(F)
Florida	18	18
Georgia	14	14
Hawaii	18	18
Idaho	18	18
Illinois	18	18
Indiana	18	18
Iowa	19	19
Kansas	18	18
Kentucky	18	18
Louisiana	16	16
Maine	18	18
Maryland	18	18
Massachusetts	18	18
Michigan	18	18
Minnesota	21	21
Mississippi	21	21
Missouri	18	18
Montana	18	18
Nebraska	19	19
Nevada	18	18
New Hampshire	18	18
New Jersey	18	18

State	To Dispose of Real Property	To Dispose of Personal Property
New Mexico	18	18
New York	18	18
North Carolina	18	18
North Dakota	18	18
Ohio	18	18
Oklahoma	18	18
Oregon	18	18
Pennsylvania	18	18
Rhode Island	18	18
South Carolina	21	21
South Dakota	18	18
Tennessee	18	18
Texas	18	18
Utah	18	18
Vermont	18	18
Virginia	18	18
Washington	18	18
West Virginia	18	18
Wisconsin	18	18
Wyoming	21	21

Copy of Actual Will in New York State

LAST WILL AND TESTAMENT

OF

I,   , residing at   , New York City, State of New York, do hereby make, publish and declare this as and for my Last Will and Testament.

First: I hereby revoke and rescind all wills and codicils heretofore made by me.

Second: I direct my Executors hereinafter named to pay my funeral expenses, the costs of administering my estate and all my just debts as soon after my decease as may be convenient, practical and proper.

Third: All the property and estate, real and personal, of whatsoever nature and wheresoever situate, of which I shall die seized or possessed, or to which at the time of my death I shall be in any manner entitled, or over which I shall have any power of appointment (all of which property is hereinafter collectively called my residuary estate), I give, devise and bequeath to my wife,   , if she shall survive me.

Fourth: If my said wife,   , shall not survive me, or if she and I die at the same time or in a common disaster, or under such circumstances that it is difficult or impossible to determine who died first, I give, devise and bequeath my residuary estate to my trustee hereinafter named, in trust, nevertheless, to divide my residuary estate into as many equal parts as shall equal in number those of my children living at my death and to hold such equal part as a separate trust fund for the benefit of each of my children who shall be living at my death. Said trustee shall collect the income therefrom and apply so much of the net income to the support, education and maintenance of the child for whom such trust fund shall have been set apart, as my trustee shall see fit, and shall accumulate, invest and reinvest the balance of said income until such child shall attain the age of eighteen (18) years, at which time all accumulations of net income and the principal of the trust fund shall be paid over to such child, and if such child shall die before attaining the age of eighteen (18) years, the then principal of the trust fund and any accumulated income shall be paid over and distributed to the issue of such child then living, in equal shares per stirpes, and if there be no such issue of mine then living, to the persons then living who would be entitled to inherit the same, in accordance with the laws of the State of New York then in force, as if I had died immediately after the death of such child, intestate, and a resident of the State of New York and owning only the said property.

If any child of mine shall have attained eighteen (18) years at the time when such trust fund is directed to be set apart for such child, my trustee shall then pay over to such child such part of such trust fund (instead of holding the same in trust) as is directed herein to be paid to such child upon attaining the age of eighteen (18) years.

If in the opinion of my trustee at the time acting, the net income from the trust created for any child of mine shall, at any time or from time to time, be insufficient for the proper support, maintenance and education of such child or for his or her comfort and welfare, I authorize and empower the trustee to use and apply all or so much of the principal of the trust hereby created for such child for such child's benefit as my trustee in her absolute discretion shall consider necessary or desirable for such purposes or any of them.

Notwithstanding anything herein contained to the contrary, if there shall be in existence trusts for more than one child of mine and if any emergency, illness or accident shall befall any of such children and if in the sole judgment and opinion of the trustee, the trust of such child or children ought not to bear the entire amount of the expenses of such emergency, illness or accident, I authorize and empower my trustee in her absolute and uncontrolled discretion to withdraw from one or more of the trusts for my other children at the time in existence hereunder all or so much of the principal thereof in equal or unequal portions as the trustee shall deem necessary or desirable for these purposes or any of them and the trustee shall be under no duty to restore such amounts so withdrawn to the principal of the trust or trusts from which such withdrawal or withdrawals have been made.

The exercise by the trustee of the discretionary powers herein granted shall be final and conclusive upon all persons interested hereunder and shall not be subject to any review.

For convenience in administration, the trustee in her absolute and uncontrolled discretion may administer in solido the assets of any trusts created hereby or any property held under a power in trust hereunder or under the last will and testament of my said wife. It is my intention, however, that a separate record shall be kept of the transactions for each separate trust or for property subject to a power in trust.

Fifth: None of my executors or trustees shall be liable for any act or omission in connection with the administration of my estate or any of the trusts or powers hereunder nor for any loss or injury to any property held in or under my estate or any of said trusts or powers, except only for his own actual fraud; and none of any executors or trustees shall be responsible for any act or omission of any other executor or trustee.

Sixth: I appoint as executrix of this will my wife,   . If for any cause, my wife,   , should not act or continue to act as executrix hereunder, I appoint as executor hereunder my friend   (currently residing at   ). I direct that no bond or security of any kind shall be required of my wife   or my friend   in any jurisdiction for the faithful performance of their duties as executors.

Seventh: Upon the death of my wife,   , I appoint as trustee of the trust or trusts created hereunder,   . I direct that no bond or security of any kind shall be required of   in any jurisdiction for the faithful performance of her duties as trustee.

Eighth: If my wife,   , should predecease me and any child of mine shall not have attained the age of eighteen (18) years at the time of my death, I appoint   (currently residing at   ) as guardian of the person and property of such minor child. I direct that no bond or other security shall be required of   in any jurisdiction for the faithful performance of her duties as guardian.

Ninth: It is my desire that my children   and   be raised in an atmosphere of understanding, tolerance and love. They should be encouraged to express themselves freely without fear. They should be allowed to explore and taste as many things as possible. They should be given flexibility, but they should always have a form and structure to their existence. They must know their own responsibilities. It is useless to try to make them understand something before they understand themselves. Their choice of religion, profession and life style should be their own. They can be exposed to certain areas, but any final decision must be their own. They must be responsible for their own actions and must never be allowed to think they may do things without regard for others. Most importantly they should be allowed to seek their own level in love and happiness.

IN WITNESS WHEREOF, I,   , have hereunto set my hand and seal this   day of   , One Thousand Nine Hundred and

Signed, sealed, published and declared by the above named Testator,
,˙as and for his Last Will and Testament, in the presence of
each of us, who, at this request, in his presence, and in the presence of each other,
have hereunto subscribed our names as attesting witnesses, the day and year last
above written.

Chapter 9   Courts and How They Work

Small Claims Courts: Notes

CLAIM LIMIT refers to the maximum amount you can sue for (according to the
latest information available). There is no minimum amount.

JURISDICTION refers to who can sue and who can be sued within the
jurisdictional limits of the particular court.

USE OF LAWYERS indicates whether the particular court bars, admits, or
limits lawyers.

MISCELLANEOUS covers additional facts to help clarify certain questions
regarding the small claims courts in your state.

ALABAMA: Claim Limit, $300; jurisdiction, district where defendant re-
sides; use of lawyers, lawyers are not required but they may appear if the
party so desires; miscellaneous, Alabama has no "small claims" courts;
hearings are usually heard before a Justice Court.

ALASKA: Claim Limit, $1,000; jurisdiction, district where defendant resides;
use of lawyers, Corporations must be represented by a lawyer; individuals
may have a lawyer present, but there is no requirement; miscellaneous,
Small Claims Court is held at the discretion of the District Court.

ARIZONA: Claim limit, $500; jurisdiction, most suits can be brought in
district where defendant resides or where problem occurred; use of lawyers,
corporations must be represented by a lawyer; individuals may have a lawyer
present, but there is no requirement; miscellaneous, Small Claims Court
known as Justice of the Peace Court.

ARKANSAS: Claim limit, $500; jurisdiction, district where defendant re-
sides; use of lawyers, not required; miscellaneous, Small Claims Court known
as Justice of Peace Court.

CALIFORNIA: Claim limit, $500; jurisdiction, district where defendant
resides or where problem occurred; use of lawyers, barred from Small Claims
Court; miscellaneous, tremendous use of Small Claims Courts throughout
California; considered one of the best judicial systems of its type in the U.S.

Federal Court System

SUPREME COURT

CIRCUIT COURTS
(U.S. Courts of Appeal)

1st	*2nd*	*3rd*	*4th*
Maine	N.Y.	N.J.	Md.
N.H.	Conn.	Pa.	Va.
Mass.	Vt.	Del.	W.Va.
R.I.		Virgin	N.C.
Puerto Rico		Islands	S.C.

5th	*6th*	*7th*	*8th*
Texas	Tenn.	Ill.	Ark.
La.	Ky.	Ind.	Iowa
Miss.	Ohio	Wis.	Minn.
Ala.	Mich.		Mo.
Ga.			Neb.
Fla.			N.D.
Canal Zone			S.D.

9th	*10th*	*D.C.*
Cal.	Colo.	Wash., D.C.
Ariz.	Kansas	
Nev.	Okla.	
Oregon	Utah	
Wash.	Wyo.	
Idaho	New Mex.	
Mont.		
Alaska		
Hawaii		
Guam		

U.S. DISTRICT COURTS

One in each State and Territory
of the U.S.

COLORADO: Claim limit, $500; jurisdiction, district where defendant resides or where obligation in question was to be performed; use of lawyers, corporations must be represented by a lawyer.

CONNECTICUT: Claim limit, $750; jurisdiction, district where either plaintiff or defendant resides; use of lawyers, not required but may appear.

DELAWARE: Claim limit, $1,500; jurisdiction, anywhere throughout State; use of lawyers, not required but may appear; miscellaneous, claims come before a Justice of the Peace.

DISTRICT OF COLUMBIA: Claim limit, $750; jurisdiction, within D.C.; use of lawyers, not required but may appear; miscellaneous, located at 613 G Street, N.W.

FLORIDA: Florida has no Small Claims Court; County Courts hear small-claims cases.

GEORGIA: Claim limit, variation all over the state; each county has its own limitation; jurisdiction, district where defendant resides; use of lawyers, not required but may appear; miscellaneous, there are Small Claims Courts and Justices of the Peace throughout the state to handle these matters; extremely varied and complicated.

HAWAII: Claim limit, $300; jurisdiction, where defendant resides of where cause of action arose; use of lawyers, not required but may appear.

IDAHO: Claim limit, $200; jurisdiction, district in which defendant resides; use of lawyers, barred.

ILLINOIS: Claim limit, $1000; jurisdiction, district in which defendant resides or where cause of action arose; use of lawyers, required only for corporations.

INDIANA: Claim limit, $500; jurisdiction, district where defendant resides; use of lawyers, required only for corporations; miscellaneous, cases comes before a Justice of the Peace.

IOWA: Claim limit, $300; jurisdiction, district where defendant resides or cause of action arose; use of lawyers, barred; miscellaneous, claims come before a Justice of the Peace.

KANSAS: Claim limit, $100; jurisdiction, district where defendant resides or where plaintiff resides if defendant also in same location at time; use of lawyers, barred.

KENTUCKY: Claim limit, $500; jurisdiction, where plaintiff or defendant resides; use of lawyers, not required but may appear; miscellaneous, cases come before a Justice of the Peace.

LOUISIANA: Claim limit, $500; jurisdiction, where defendant resides; use of lawyers, not required but may appear; miscellaneous, comes before Justice of the Peace except in New Orleans, where matters go before the City Court.

MAINE: Claim limit, $200; jurisdiction, where either plaintiff or defendant resides; use of lawyers, not required but may appear.

MARYLAND: Claim limit, $1000; jurisdiction, where defendant resides or does business; use of lawyers, not required but may appear.

MASSACHUSETTS: Claim limit, $400; jurisdiction, district where defendant resides or does business; use of lawyers, not required but may appear.

MICHIGAN: Claim limit, $500; depending on area; it varies from $300 to $500 throughout state; jurisdiction, where defendant resides; use of lawyers, not required but may appear; miscellaneous, range is from $300 to $500 throughout state; generally higher in cities.

MINNESOTA: Claim limit, $500; depending on area; jurisdiction, district where defendant resides; if defendant not a resident, then it applies to where plaintiff resides; use of lawyers, barred.

MISSISSIPPI: Claim limit, $200; jurisdiction, district in which defendant resides or where cause of action arose; use of lawyers, not required but may appear; miscellaneous, cases come before a Justice of the Peace.

MISSOURI: Claim limit, varies throughout the state from county to county; jurisdiction, district where defendant resides or where plaintiff resides *and* defendant is within that jurisdiction; use of lawyers, not required but may appear; miscellaneous, cases come before a Magistrate's Court with limits of from $2000 to $3500.

MONTANA: Claim limit, $300; jurisdiction, where defendant resides; use of lawyers, not required but may appear; miscellaneous, cases come before a Justice's Court.

NEBRASKA: Claim limit, $500; jurisdiction, district where defendant resides or cause of action arose; use of lawyers, barred; miscellaneous, cases come before a Justice of the Peace or some municipal courts within the larger cities.

NEVADA: Claim limit, $300; jurisdiction, where defendant resides; use of lawyers, not required but may appear.

NEW HAMPSHIRE: Claim limit, $300; jurisdiction, where either plaintiff or defendant resides; use of lawyers, not required but may appear.

NEW JERSEY: Claim limit, $200; jurisdiction, where defendant resides; use of lawyers, not required but may appear.

NEW MEXICO: Claim limit, $2000; jurisdiction, district where defendant resides or where cause of action arose; use of lawyers, not required but may appear.

NEW YORK: Claim limit, $1000; jurisdiction, county where defendant resides; In New York City, Small Claims Court applies to defendants who have an office or who are employed within the city; use of lawyers, corporations must be represented by a lawyer; individuals may use lawyers but are not required to do so.

NORTH CAROLINA: Claim limit, $300; jurisdiction, district where defendant resides or where cause of action arose; use of lawyers, not required but may appear.

NORTH DAKOTA: Claim limit, $200; jurisdiction, district where defendant resides; use of lawyers, not required but may appear.

OHIO: Claim limit, $150; jurisdiction, district where defendant resides or where cause of action arose; use of lawyers, not required but may appear.

OKLAHOMA: Claim limit, $400; jurisdiction, place where cause of action arose; use of lawyers, not required but may appear.

OREGON: Claim limit, $500, jurisdiction, district where defendant is located; use of lawyers, only if court agrees.

PENNSYLVANIA: Claim limit, $500; jurisdiction, place where defendant is located or where cause of action arose; use of lawyers, not required but may appear; corporations must be represented by lawyer in Philadelphia court.

PUERTO RICO: Claim limit, $2500; jurisdiction, place where cause of action arose; use of lawyers, not required but may appear.

RHODE ISLAND: Claim limit, $300; jurisdiction, district where either plaintiff or defendant resides; use of lawyers, mandatory when plaintiffs are corporations.

SOUTH CAROLINA: Claim limit, $1000; jurisdiction, district where defendant resides or where cause of action arose; use of lawyers, not required but may appear; miscellaneous, cases come before a Magistrate's Court.

SOUTH DAKOTA: Claim limit, $500; jurisdiction, district where defendant resides or where cause of action arose; use of lawyers, no limitations.

TENNESSEE: Claim limit, $3000; jurisdiction, district where defendant resides or where cause of action arose; use of lawyers, not required but may appear; miscellaneous, cases come before a Justice of the Peace.

TEXAS: Claim limit, $200; jurisdiction, district where defendant resides or where cause of action arose; use of lawyers, not required but may appear.

UTAH: Claim limit, $200; jurisdiction, district where defendant resides or where cause of action arose; use of lawyers, not required but may appear.

VIRGIN ISLANDS: Claim limit, $300; jurisdiction, place where defendant is found; use of lawyers, barred.

VERMONT: Claim limit, $250; jurisdiction, district where defendant resides; use of lawyers, not required but may appear.

VIRGINIA: Claim limit, $3000; jurisdiction, district where defendant resides or where cause of action arose; use of lawyers, not required but may appear; miscellaneous, cases come before an entity known as Courts Not of Record.

WASHINGTON: Claim limit, $200; jurisdiction, district where defendant resides or where cause of action arose; use of lawyers, barred unless with court's permission.

WEST VIRGINIA: Claim limit, $300; jurisdiction, district where defendant resides or cause of action arose; use of lawyers, not required but may appear; miscellaneous, cases come before a Justice of the Peace.

WISCONSIN: Claim limit, $500; jurisdiction, district where defendant resides or where cause of action arose; use of lawyers, not required but may appear.

WYOMING: Claim limit, $100; jurisdiction, district where defendant resides or where cause of action arose; use of lawyers, not required but may appear; miscellaneous, cases come before a Justice of the Peace.

American Arbitration Association Regional Offices

ARIZONA
Security Center, Suite 669
222 North Central Avenue
Phoenix 85004
(602) 252-7357

CALIFORNIA
443 Shatto Place
Los Angeles 90020
(213) 383-6516

San Diego Trust & Savings Bank
  Building
Suite 909
530 Broadway
San Diego 92102
(714) 239-3051

690 Market Street, Suite 800
San Francisco 94104
(415) 981-3901

CONNECTICUT

37 Lewis Street, Room 406
Hartford 06103
(203) 278-6000

DISTRICT OF COLUMBIA

1730 Rhode Island Avenue, N.W.
Suite 509
Washington 20036
(202) 296-8510

FLORIDA

2250 S.W. Third Avenue
Miami 33129
(305) 854-1616

GEORGIA

Equitable Building
100 Peachtree Street
Atlanta 30303
(404) 788-4151

ILLINOIS

180 N. LaSalle Street
Suite 1025
Chicago 60601
(312) 346-2282

MASSACHUSETTS

294 Washington Street
Boston 02108
(617) 542-1071

MICHIGAN

City National Bank Building
Suite 1234
645 Griswold Street
Detroit 48226
(313) 964-2525

MINNESOTA

Foshay Tower, Suite 1001
821 Marquette Avenue
Minneapolis 55402
(612) 335-6545

NEW JERSEY

96 Bayard Street
New Brunswick 08901
(201) 247-6080

NEW YORK

585 Stewart Avenue
Garden City 11530
(516) 222-1660

140 West 51st Street
New York City 10020
(212) 977-2090

731 James Street
Syracuse 13203
(315) 472-5483

NEW YORK—cont.

34 S. Broadway/5th Floor
White Plains 10601
(914) 946-1119

NORTH CAROLINA

3235 Eastway Drive
Suite 205
Charlotte 28218
(704) 568-5420

OHIO

Carew Tower, Suite 2308
441 Vine Street
Cincinnati 45202
(513) 241-8434

215 Euclid Avenue, Room 930
Cleveland 44114
(216) 241-4741

PENNSYLVANIA

1520 Locust Street, 12th Floor
Philadelphia 19102
(215) 732-5260

Two Gateway Center
Pittsburgh 15222
(412) 261-3617

TEXAS

Praetorian Building
Suite 1115
1607 Main Street
Dallas 75201
(214) 748-4979

WASHINGTON

Central Building, Room 310
810 Third Avenue
Seattle 98104
(206) 622-6435

Community Dispute Services of AAA

CALIFORNIA

443 Shatto Place
Los Angeles 90020
(213) 383-6683

690 Market Street, Suite 800
San Francisco 94104
(415) 981-3901

DISTRICT OF COLUMBIA

1730 Rhode Island Avenue, N.W.
Suite 509
Washington 20036
(202) 296-8510 and 296-2533

MASSACHUSETTS

294 Washington Street
Boston 02108
(617) 542-2278

NEW YORK

36 West Main Street, Room 410
Rochester 14614
(716) 546-5110

OHIO

177 S. Broadway Street, Room 438
Akron 44308
(216) 762-8636

215 Euclid Avenue, Room 930
Cleveland 44114
(216) 241-4741

Arbitration

If you decide to arbitrate a dispute, you may have to fill out a form similar to these Demand for Arbitration forms, which are used in New York State in order to commence an arbitration proceeding under the jurisdiction of the American Arbitration Association. Form "A" covers accident cases, and Form "B" is for general commercial use.

For Use in New York State

AMERICAN ARBITRATION ASSOCIATION

Accident Claims Rules—Demand for Arbitration

(Company) _____ *Date:*
(Address of Claims Office) _____
(City and State) _____

PLEASE TAKE NOTICE that the filing party, a party to an Insurance Policy providing for protection against loss due to personal injuries sustained in accidents involving Uninsured or Hit-and-Run Motorists which provides for arbitration of disputes arising thereunder in accordance with the Rules of the American Arbitration Association, hereby demands arbitration thereunder.

Issuing Company: _____
Name of Policyholder: _____
Policy Number: _____Effective Dates: _____ to _____
Claim Number: _____

Name(s) of Claimant(s)	*Check, if a Minor*	*Amount Claimed*
	☐	
	☐	
	☐	
	☐	
	☐	
	☐	

Date of Accident: _____ Location: _____
                                        (City and State)

CHECK ONE: Uninsured Motorist ☐   Hit-and-Run ☐

Nature of Injuries:

Hearing Locale Requested: _____
                                        (City and State)

You are hereby notified that copies of our Arbitration Agreement and of this Demand are being filed with the American Arbitration Association at its _____ Regional Office, with the request that it commence the administration of the arbitration.

PLEASE TAKE FURTHER NOTICE that unless within ten days after service of this Notice of Intention to Arbitrate, you apply to stay the arbitration herein, you shall thereafter be precluded from objecting that a valid agreement was not made or has not been complied with and from asserting in court the bar of a limitation of time.

Signed _____

(May be signed by Attorney)

Name, address and telephone number of Attorney:

Name and address of the party serving the notice:

_____

_____

_____

_____

_____

_____

Three copies of this Demand should be filed with a regional office of the AAA, together with two copies of the Uninsured Motorist Endorsement. Another copy should be sent to the claims office with which previous negotiations have been conducted. The administrative fee of $50 should accompany the initiating papers.

For Use in New York State

AMERICAN ARBITRATION ASSOCIATION

Commercial Arbitration Rules Demand for Arbitration

Date:

TO:

(Name) _____

(of party upon whom the Demand is made)

(Address) _____

(City and State) _____

Named claimant, a party to an arbitration agreement contained in a written contract, dated _____, providing for arbitration, hereby demands arbitration thereunder.

(attach arbitration clause or quote hereunder)

Nature of Dispute:

Claim or Relief Sought: (amount, if any)

PLEASE TAKE FURTHER NOTICE, that unless within twenty days after service of this Notice of Intention to Arbitrate, you apply to stay the arbitration herein, you shall thereafter be precluded from objecting that a valid agreement was not made or has not been complied with and from asserting in court the bar of a limitation of time.

HEARING LOCALE REQUESTED: _____
(City and State)

You are hereby notified that copies of our arbitration agreement and of this demand are being filed with the American Arbitration Association at its _____ Regional Office, with the request that it commence the administration of the arbitration. Under Section 7 of the Commercial Arbitration Rules, you may file an answering statement within seven days after notice from the Administrator.

Signed _____
(May be Signed by Attorney)

Name of Claimant _____
Address (to be used
in connection with this case) _____
City and State _____ Zip Code _____
Telephone _____

To institute proceedings, please send two copies of this Demand with the administrative fee, as provided in Section 47 of the Rules.

Chapter 10:   Selecting a Lawyer

NATIONAL BAR ASSOCIATION

American Bar Association
1155 East 60th Street
Chicago, IL 60637
(312) 947-3930

STATE BAR ASSOCIATIONS

ALABAMA

P.O. Box 606
Tallassee 36078
(205) 283-3533

ALASKA

210 Nerland Building
Fairbanks 99701
(907) 452-4215

ARIZONA

Suite 403
11 West Jefferson
Phoenix 85003
(602) 254-8861

ARKANSAS

400 West Markham
Little Rock 72201
(501) 375-4605

CALIFORNIA

601 McAllister Street
San Francisco 94102
(415) 922-1440

COLORADO

200 West Fourteenth Avenue
Denver 80204
(303) 222-9421

CONNECTICUT

15 Lewis Street
Hartford 06103
(203) 249-9141

DELAWARE

1207 King Street
Wilmington 19801
(302) 658-0847

DISTRICT OF COLUMBIA

1426 H Street, N.W.
Washington 20005
(202) 638-1500

FLORIDA

The Florida Bar Center
Tallahassee 32304
(904) 222-5286

GEORGIA

1510 Fulton National Bank
   Building
Atlanta 30303
(404) 522-6255

HAWAII

P.O. Box 26
Honolulu 96810
(808) 537-1868

IDAHO

P.O. Box 895
Boise 83701
(208) 342-8958

ILLINOIS

Illinois Bar Center
Springfield 62701
(217) 525-1760

INDIANA

230 East Ohio
Indianapolis 46204
(317) 639-5465

IOWA

1101 Fleming Building
Des Moines 50309
(515) 243-3179

KANSAS

P.O. Box 1037
Topeka 66601
(913) 234-5696

KENTUCKY

315 West Main Street
Frankfort 40601
(502) 564-3795

LOUISIANA

225 Barrone Street, Suite 210
New Orleans 70112
(504) 566-1600

MAINE

P.O. Box 788
Augusta 04330
(207) 622-7523

MARYLAND

905 Keyser Building
Baltimore 21202
(301) 685-7878

MASSACHUSETTS

One Center Plaza
Boston 02108
(617) 523-4529

MICHIGAN

306 Townsend Street
Lansing 48933
(517) 372-9030

MINNESOTA

100 Minnesota Federal Building
Minneapolis 55402
(612) 335-1183

MISSISSIPPI

620 North State Street
Jackson 39201
(601) 948-4471

MISSOURI

P.O. Box 119
Jefferson City 65101
(314) 635-4128

MONTANA

P.O. Box 4669
Helena 59601
(406) 442-7660

NEBRASKA

1019 Sharp Building
Lincoln 68508
(402) 475-7091

NEVADA

P.O. Box 2125
Reno 89505
(702) 323-0338

NEW HAMPSHIRE

77 Market Street
Manchester 03101
(603) 669-4869

NEW JERSEY

172 West State Street
Trenton 08608
(609) 394-1101

NEW MEXICO

1117 Stanford, N.E.
Albuquerque 87131
(505) 842-3901

NEW YORK

One Elk Street
Albany 12207
(518) 445-1211

NORTH CAROLINA

P.O. Box 25850
Raleigh 27611
(919) 828-4620

NORTH DAKOTA

P.O. Box 2136
Bismarck 58501
(701) 255-1404

OHIO

33 West Eleventh Avenue
Columbus 43201
(614) 421-2121

OKLAHOMA

P.O. Box 53036
Oklahoma City 73105
(405) 524-2365

OREGON

1776 S.W. Madison
Portland 97205
(503) 229-5788

PENNSYLVANIA

Twelfth Floor
Packard Building
Philadelphia 19102
(215) 569-4000

PUERTO RICO

P.O. Box 1900
San Juan 00903
(809) 724-3358

RHODE ISLAND

1804 Industrial Bank Building
Providence 02903
(401) 421-5740

SOUTH CAROLINA

P.O. Box 11297
Columbia 29211
(803) 779-6653

SOUTH DAKOTA

222 East Capitol
Pierre 57501
(605) 224-7554

TENNESSEE

1717 West End Avenue
Suite 600
Nashville 37023
(615) 329-1601

TEXAS

1200 One Main Place
Dallas 75250
(214) 747-9211

UTAH

425 East First South
Salt Lake City 84101
(801) 322-1015

VERMONT

P.O. Box 100
Montpelier 05602
(802) 223-2020

VIRGINIA

700 East Main Street
Richmond 23219
(804) 786-2061

WASHINGTON

505 Madison
Seattle 98104
(206) 622-6054

WEST VIRGINIA

E-404, State Capitol
Charleston 25322
(304) 346-8414

WISCONSIN

402 West Wilson Street
Madison 53703
(608) 257-3838

WYOMING

P.O. Box 3388
Cheyenne 82001
(307) 632-9061

LOCAL BAR ASSOCIATIONS

ARIZONA

County Bar Association
3033 North Central Avenue
Phoenix 85012
(602) 277-2366

CALIFORNIA

Alameda County
405 Fourteenth Street
Suite 208
Oakland 94612
(415) 893-7160

Beverly Hills
1800 Century Park East
Los Angeles 90067
(213) 553-6822

Los Angeles
606 South Olive Street
Suite 1212
Los Angeles 90014
(213) 620-6200

Orange County
1055 North Main Street
Suite 801
Santa Ana 92701
(714) 835-3338

San Diego
1200 Third Avenue
San Diego 92101
(714) 231-0781

San Francisco
220 Bush Street
Twenty-first Floor
San Francisco 94104
(415) 392-3960

Santa Clara
111 North Market Street
San Jose 95113
(408) 288-8840

COLORADO

Denver
200 West Fourteenth Avenue
Denver 80204
(303) 222-9421

FLORIDA

Dade County
111 N.W. First Avenue
Miami 33128
(305) 379-0641

GEORGIA

Atlanta
2400 First National Bank
Atlanta 30303
(404) 658-1200

ILLINOIS

Cook County
29 South LaSalle Street
Suite 1040
Chicago 60603
(312) 782-7348

INDIANA

Indianapolis
One Indiana Square, Suite 2550
Indianapolis 46204
(317) 632-8240

KENTUCKY

Louisville
400 Court House
Louisville 40202
(502) 583-5314

MARYLAND

Baltimore City
621 Court House
Baltimore 21202
(301) 539-5936

MASSACHUSETTS

Boston
100 Federal Street
Boston 02110
(617) 357-9300

MICHIGAN

Detroit
600 Woodward Avenue
Law Center
Detroit 48226
(313) 961-3545

MINNESOTA

Minneapolis
700 Cargill Building
Minneapolis 55402
(612) 338-5336

MISSOURI

Kansas City
510 Bryant Building
1102 Grand
Kansas City 64106
(816) 474-4322

Metropolitan St. Louis
One Mercantile Center
Suite 3600
St. Louis 63101
(314) 421-4134

NEW JERSEY

Essex County
92 Washington Street
Newark 07102
(201) 622-6207

NEW YORK

City of New York
42 West Forty-fourth Street
New York 10036
(212) 682-0606

OHIO

Greater Cleveland
118 St. Clair Avenue
Cleveland 44114
(216) 696-3525

Cincinnati
Suite 400
26 East Sixth Street
Cincinnati 45202
(513) 381-8213

Columbus
66 South Third Street
Columbus 43215
(614) 221-4112

Cayahoga County
305 Women's Federal Building
Cleveland 44114
(216) 621-5112

OKLAHOMA

Oklahoma County
311 North Harvey
Oklahoma City 73102
(405) 236-8421

Tulsa County
822 Beacon Building
Tulsa 74103
(918) 584-5243

OREGON

Multnomah County
910 Pacific Building
Portland 97204
(503) 228-8271

PENNSYLVANIA

Allegheny County
920 City Building
Pittsburgh 15219
(412) 288-3146

Philadelphia
City Hall Annex
Room 423
Philadelphia 19107
(215) 686-5687

TEXAS

Dallas
Adolphus Hotel
Dallas 75221
(214) 742-4675

TEXAS—cont.

Houston
200 Houston Bar Center Building
Houston 77002
(713) 222-1444

WASHINGTON

Seattle-King County
320 Central Building
Seattle 98104
(206) 623-2551

WISCONSIN

Milwaukee
740 North Plankinton Avenue
Milwaukee 53203
(414) 271-3833

Contact the Executive Director or Executive Secretary at the above addresses for further information.

Index

Adoptions, 32–35
  "black market," 34
  private, 33
  through state agencies, 33
Alimony, 36–37
Annulment, of marriage, 35
Antenuptial agreements, 31
Apartment rentals, 44–50
  breaking leases, 47
  collective non-payment, 48
  eviction, 47
  security deposits, 48–49
  signing leases, 45
Arbitration
  procedures, 116–119
  regional offices, 177–181
Arraignment, 72
Arrest warrant, 76–77
Assault and battery, 21
Automobile accidents, 81–87

Bail, 72
"Bait and switch" practice, 8
"Balloon payment," 13
Bankruptcy, 63, 66–67
Bar Associations, national, state and
  local, 181–187

Binders, 52
Business relationships, 60–69
  corporations, 63–65
  individual ownership, 60–61
  partnerships, 61–63
  terminations, 65–66

Canons of Ethics, 122–126
Certificate of Incorporation, 64
Child custody, 37–38
Child support, 37
Citizen's arrest procedure, 77
Civil law, 76
Civil Rights Act, 24, 27
Closings, on houses, 53–55
Codicils, to wills, 95, 102
Community property laws, 31, 38,
  105–106
Computer errors, correcting, 13–15
Condominiums, 55–56
Consumer protection, 4–18
  credit, 11–17
  deceptive practices, 7–9
  federal regulation, 9–11
  product liability, 17–18
  warranties, 6
Consumer Protection Credit Act, 11

Consumer protection organizations, 139–153
Contingent fee arrangement, 18
Contract to buy, 5
Contract of sale, 5
Cooperatives, 57–58
Copyright, 67–68
Corporations, forming and dissolving, 63–66
Courts, 108–119
  federal, 108–110
  small claims, 112–116, 171–176
  state, 110–111
Credit, 11–15
Credit bureaus, 15–16
Crimes, 70–80
  arrest and search warrants, 76–79
  bail, 72
  hearings, 72–76
  rights of accused, 70–72
Criminal law, 76
Custody of children, 37–38

Deeds to property, 54
Defamation of character, 21–22
Divorce, 35–43
  alimony, 36–37
  child support, 37
  custody, 37–38
  "friendly," 36
  no-fault, 39–40
  property division in, 38
  "quickie," 40–41
  self-representation in, 42–43
  state requirements for, 158–162
Divorce decree, 35
"Doing business as," in sole proprietorship, 60
Door-to-door sales, 14
Double jeopardy, 21
Due process of law, 20

Equal Credit Opportunity Act, 27
Equal Employment Opportunity Commission, 25
Equal opportunities
  credit, 27
  employment, 24–27
  housing, 27

Equal Pay Act, 26
Equal Rights Amendment, 26
Estate planning, 101–102
Executors, 98, 100–101
Express warranty, 6

Fair Credit Reporting Act, 15
Fair Employment Practices Act, 25
Family matters, 29–43
  adoption, 32
  alimony, 36–37
  annulment, 35
  child custody, 37–38
  child support, 37
  common-law marriages, 30
  damage incurred by children, 32
  divorce, 36–43
  interracial marriages, 30
  premarital agreements, 31
  property division, in divorce, 38
  separation agreements, 36–38
  state requirements for divorce, 158–162
  voidable marriages, 35–36
Federal Communications Commission, 16
Federal Register, 23
Federal regulatory agencies, 9–11, 144, 148–152
Federal Trade Commission, 6, 9
Freedom of assembly, 20
Freedom of press, 23
Freedom of religion, 20
Freedom of speech, 20
Fees, legal, 18, 90–91, 131–135
Felonies, 74, 76
Finance charges, 11–12
Food and Drug Administration, 9, 10

Gambling contracts, 5
Garnishment of wages, 16
Gay rights, 26
Gifts, engagement and wedding, 30–31
Grand juries, 74

Habeas Corpus, 21
Handwritten wills. *See* Holographic wills

Hearings, 72–76
Hit-and-run accidents, 86
Holographic wills
  legality of, 99
  preparation of, 96
  state requirements for, 166–167
Homes, buying and selling
  bargain and sale deed, 54
  binders or purchase agreements,
    52
  closing, 54–55
  contracts of sale, 53
  full covenant and warranty deed,
    54
  insurance and liability, 87–90
  lawyer in, 50–52
  quitclaim deed, 54
  title, 53
  title insurance, 54
  title searches, 54
Human rights, 19–28, 153–156. *See
  also* specific rights and freedoms

Implied warranty, 6
Indictments, 73
Invasion of privacy, 22–24

"Knock" rule, 77

Landlord-tenant relations, 44–50
Lawyers, 120–138
  ethics, 120–126
  expected results, 135–137
  fees, 131–135
  selecting, 126–128
  types, 128–131
Leases, in renting property, 44–46
Legal fees, 90–91
Liability insurance, 88
Libel, 22
Licensing agencies for controlling
  occupations or professions, 9
Local legislative control, 7–9

Magnuson-Moss Warranty Act, 10
Marriages, 29–32. *See also* Family
  matters
  common-law, 30
  interracial, 30

void, 35
voidable, 36
Medical malpractice, 91–94
  attorney's services in, 92, 93–94
  definition of, 91
  wrongful death in, 92–93
Miranda v Arizona, 71
Misdemeanors, 74, 76
Mistrials, 74

Name changing
  procedure, 28
  sample name-change petition, 157
National Environmental Protection
  Act, 11
Negligence
  automobile, 81–87
  home, 87–90
No-fault
  divorce, 39–40
  insurance, 82–86

Ownership
  of consumer goods, 5
  individual, of business, 60
  of real property, 44–59

Partnerships, business
  articles of, 63
  debts incurred, 62–63
  general, 62
  investment in, 62–63
  limited, 62
  profit division, 62
  termination of, 65
Patents, 67–68
Premarital contracts, 31–32
Probate, of wills, 96–97
Product liability, 17
Public policy, 5, 31, 45
Punitive damages, 10, 22

Real property, 44–59. *See also*
  specific type, e.g., Homes,
  Condominiums, Cooperatives
Renting, 44–50
Repossession of consumer goods, 15
Retail Installment Credit Agreement,
  12

Retainer agreements, 132
Right to hold public office, 20
Right of Privacy Law, 23
Right to vote, 20

Search and seizure, 21
Search warrants, 78
Security deposits, 48
Self-incrimination
    in arrest and arraignment, 75
    and martyrdom, 79
    protection against, in testimony, 21
Separation agreements, 35–36
Serious injury, in automobile
        negligence, 83
Slander, 22
Small Business Association, 162–166
Small claims courts, 48–50, 89–90,
        112–116
Small criminal complaints, 78–79
Sole proprietorship, 60–61
"Stop and frisk" laws, 77
Subchapter S Corporation
        arrangement, 64
Subscription agreements, in purchase
        of cooperatives, 58

Terminating a business
    bankruptcy, 66–67
    corporations, 65–66
    individual proprietorships, 65
    partnerships, 65–66

Title to property, 53–54
    insurance, 54
    searches, 54
Trademarks, 67–68
Trial by jury, right to, 74
Trusts
    in estate planning, 103–104
    revocable and irrevocable, 104
    and tax laws, 103
    testamentary and living, 104
Truth-in-Lending Act, 11, 13, 14, 16,
        27

Uniform Commercial Code, 4
Uniform Consumer Credit Act, 13
Uniform Sales Act, 4

Violation, length of imprisonment for,
        76

Warranties, 6–7
    express, 6
    implied, 6
Wills, 65, 95–107
    alternatives to, 102–105
    benefits of, 97–98
    challenges to, 105–106
    estate planning, 101–102
    requirements of, 99–101, 166–171
Wrongful death, in medical
        malpractice, 92–93